SELECTIVE MEMORY,
VERY SELECTIVE

PAULO CASTRO

Quantum
Discovery
A LITERARY AGENCY

Selective Memory, Very Selective
Copyright © 2024 by Paulo Castro

ISBN
978-1-963254-37-2 (Paperback)
978-1-963254-38-9 (eBook)

DEDICATION

I dedicate this work to the two people who contributed immensely to the construction of myself.

To my father, who even without many words and despite all our differences, always took good care of me, and without hesitating, always attended to my needs and requests, with much love and affection.

And to my mom. Beyond her dedication and support at all times, she has always challenged me, showing me possibilities, and encouraging me saying that with faith and hard work, I could be and do anything I wanted.

Like me, she also loves to write and her greatest contribution to this book, aside from helping me write properly, or more sophisticatedly, were the moments of free conversation we shared every morning joking about the meaning of several words and mistakes we noticed in advertises and notes written on the walls along many streets we use to cross in our city in Brazil.

Those things undoubtedly stimulated my imagination and infected me with the desire to write.

TABLE OF CONTENTS

FOREWORD

I am pleased to have the privilege of making the exordium for this first Paulo's literary essay. His name already inspires the memory of the great warrior who was Saul, a persecutor of Christians until Christ himself, looking at his heart saw the full dimension of courage that existed there and with a bolt of lightning made him fall from his powerful horse, interpolating him: Saul, Saul, why are you persecuting me? And Saul became Paul from that moment on, the strong great apostle of Christ, who wrote in one of his letters: "Even though I speak all languages of the world but do not have love in my heart, my life would be meaningless." So, Paul, your mother had a lot of wisdom when named you after the apostle Paul.

As yourself said, you was born looking like an alien, which is clearly an exaggeration. Maybe you have not arisen in the world very cute, but people change as they grow, so today you are a handsome, smart, and intelligent young man and most important, full of love.

In this book, Paulo takes us through all his experiences and well-lived years, whether in Brazil or in the United States. This book is about the adventures of a boy who had been compared to a frog by himself and some friends but then, slowly paraded girlfriends, loves, hidden kisses… Aline, Amanda, Larissa, Dafna… and many others…

But life is not only made of love and pleasures. Paulo, amid so many happy adventures, also finds unpleasantness and suffering. Among them, he tells us about a very traumatic motorcycle accident where divine providence allowed him to survive.

It was a few years after this sad moment that we met at UNIFACEX University that became part of his life as well register in this book that, for being the first, holds great promise.

Now Paulo have graduated in Psychology, and the market needs to find his potential as a professional and a writer with a very easy style, correct, with picaresque trend. This book is a vision of life where love merges with the joy of living.

It was pleasurable to read this work and write these introductory words. Those who also read it will certainly be rewarded with great pleasure. I recommend it!

Prof. Raimundo Vieira

ACKNOWLEDGEMENTS

To start with, I want to thank everyone who told me, "Your life could become a nice book." I believed in what they were joking about. And they were right.

I also want to thank the girls who inspired me to flirt and romances and friends who are part of my story.

It is also important to honor people who have contributed to producing this book: Prof. Raimundo Vieira, dean of UNIFACEX and great friend, who with generosity and attention, used his precious time to write the foreword of this work. the Professor, and also a friend, Rejane who with her experience, grace and sympathy reviewed and updated my text. And Professor José Maria Barreto de Figueiredo, CEO of CIFE, who always believed in my potential and enabled the printing the first version of this book in my native language, Portuguese.

Finally, my siblings, Andre, Lyslei and Fábio, for the unconditional love they have always shown, and also for the many life experiences we shared that marked my memories.

CHAPTER 1

How It Was In The Beginning

Does life really begin at birth time, or when we start making our choices? Because in the beginning, we are still choices of our parents, yet sometimes not even that, since, usually, most of the time we are born just as a result of an accidental natural act.

Who knows? Who could say? What for? It will not change anything anyways, it's done, and we were already born.

Many people say that babies are chubby, cute, funny looking, adorable, and delicious, hum... bull S...In my case, because I was sitting in my mom's belly, I was born with a flat head in such a way that the ears would go over my head. I heard reports calling me Dr. Spock - that extraterrestrial from Star Trek ... It must be true because they have not had the courage to take pictures, thank goodness. If it was not for this book, no one would ever know that detail. It was a Family ultra-secret subject.

Over time, miraculously, the head smoothed out and I became a baby all rounded, really fine... this time I had dozens of witnesses to prove that. But the funny thing is that everything that is good, does not last forever. I grew up and changed. My legs that had several bumps of a cute chunk baby now seemed like a fishing rod, so thin. When I turned sideways, they would disappear. So sad! My arms, just like the legs, just bones, nothing else. When I noticed, I had experienced several metamorphoses - ET, the baby cuddly and at eleven, I was looking like a frog!

As my mother always said, and until today says, "age is a disease, crippling, irreversible and fatal." Of course, she refers to old age, but in my case, the transition from child to teenager had the same effect, excluding going up to the fatal term, but with an emphasis on deforming.

It was not easy. I could not accept leaving my baby cuteness behind and also that super delicious little boy, to end up being something of long arms, thin legs, fluffy and fallen belly! I was fit, but my belly was nasty. It was all alright! I was growing. The transformation was inevitable.

I would have to adapt to my new look. After all, I was just like my friends.

But that was later, I haven't got there yet. For now, I just remember that pile of strangers, undefined forms, like me, singing the school and national anthem every morning. It was the beginning of primary school. An evolution of what my grandmother called school group, but not as pretentious as elementary school nowadays.

Today, I think that singing hymns at the time of entry in schools, before starting the classes is super valuable. But at the time, it was purely boring. It was, in the words of my aunt, it is like a wrist cut.

Despite the pathetic ritual, since no one understood what we were saying, I loved going to school. Do not get me wrong, I said I loved going to school, not studying. But I was always lucky, despite my strange look as a teenager, most of the other boys was even worse than me. It made me the leader. Rarely had to do the homework, the girls always helped.

Thanks to God my ability to communicate has always been one of my best features. I could definitely say, I was not the most handsome, even less the most attractive, but I always enjoyed writing, and since my childhood I wrote romantic verses, poems, or just little things girls loved to listen to. I think I remember one of those things. (Keep in mind that I was only eleven or twelve, just a child) - "If I was you, and you were me, I would be you and you, me. But, as I'm me and you are you, I will love you and you will love me too"!

A pearl of children's literature! For these and some other things I did back then, I always ended up well with the girls. I really loved those girls!

Of course, at school, life wasn't always easy. I always paid attention in class and attended all the activities. Since I was not a very good student, at least, I pleased the teachers and the smart girls. I was so slick, or in a Brazilian expression (*cara de pau* / wooden *face)* that seemed I was carved out a soap, not born as every child. However, because of that I was very popular, and always graduated year after year … always in evidence, thanks to my darling girls and nice teachers, of course!

Yeah, but it was not all nice at all the time wonderful. Classes, work quizzes, tests, I was always doing well, however, we still had to go for physical education classes, the best thing for every kid, including me. Sometimes!

I can't denial I loved to run, jump, play ball, and do jumping jacks, push-ups and whatever else, all with a lot of disposition and excitement. I also would do all the tasks in the classes, on time and better than expected, just to be ready to play ball, the most waited moment, but always hoping never to be cast in the shirtless team.

But one day, my nightmare happened. I almost gave up playing. You now might be wondering why. But maybe you are not remembering my body description - legs and arms that couldn't even be seen if I turned sideways, fallen boobies and fluffy belly?

The time of the physical education class was just before the break recess and sometimes the break started, and we were still in the game. At this time, every child of all the other classes would go rushing to the court to see the end of the game and wait to enter the court to play as well. Of course, that horrible day I was in a shirtless team. And a boy named Joseph, skinny and tall, pointed me shouting:

_"Go for it (*MARIA PEITUDA / Mary big boobies)*

It was traumatic! I tried in every way to reverse the situation, calling him a stick-stick, toothpick, fishing rod, stick, insect, among millions more, but Mary big boobies got stock in everybody's head. Everyone that wanted to make fun of me called me that! But the fishing rod and insect also became his nicknames. Later we became best friends. The funny thing is that Joseph and I started to introduce ourselves as: Mary big bust and fishing rod.

Thanks God I changed schools the following year UFFA!

New school, new people, new and forgotten nicknames and friends … I was lucky. But I knew that everything could happen again in a simple gym class.

I loved it too much not to participate. I had to live with that risk…

In this new school, that I still remember the name, Santa Barbara, the routine was similar: boring lectures, girlfriends to assist in the tasks and recreational activities shortly after the class of physical education. It seemed likely my humiliation would happen all over again. But no, there were two uniforms for Physical Education: blue shirts and white shirts, school colors. Was it pure luck, or God's provision?

In that new school, my reputation was saved. Maria Busty never more. if Joseph ever spoke to someone about it, I would kill him with my bare hands, without any remorse.

In that school I met Aline, who at the time I called, without any doubt, my first love.

Certainly, I did not yet know the magnitude of true love, but for me she was better than perfect. More beautiful than the flowers bloom, more radiant than the light from the sun. I looked at her and she said *Hi*. It took me a few seconds to respond. She must have thought, at first, I had some mental dysfunction.

After I recovered from that first moment of surprise, I started using all the communication skills I had and even some I did not have yet. That HI was the most beautiful word of my life until that moment, obviously.

After that first HI, we started talking every day and spending time together between and after classes, sharing opinions, telling jokes, and laughing a lot. For me nothing in the world was the same. It was funny that her HI was always on my mind - her voice, her expression, and beautiful smile. I was feeling something new, different. I needed to go further. I knew I would need something more powerful, stronger to forget the blessed HI. Actually, not to forget it, replace it briefly. One day, after accompanying her home from school, and before saying goodbye, I stole a pop kiss, and ran. It was instantaneous, I couldn't think of the HI no more, it was a really fast stolen pop kiss, but it was the first. And amazingly good!

The next day we talked about the kiss and laughed a little, it had been the first to both of us, uffa! She was a little shy, but it was good, simple, tasty, and unforgettable. We did not need anything else, just keeping on doing it every day.

Life was "bótima", using a word of a future girlfriend, in Portuguese. It is a mix of good and really good! But as an old expression says, everything that's good does not last long, soon I had to move again!

I was devastated. I did not want to change schools. It was all going very well: first girlfriend, lots of friends, no disagreement with anyone and I lived close to the school, which avoided daddy's company to get there. It gave me some independence. Perfect! Everything was better than perfect.

Why ruin everything moving again? I did not know the reasons: was it because of Dad's work or problems with the rent of our house? The reality was cruel: another house in another neighborhood.

Another life! What I wanted did not matter. I was only fourteen or less.

ANOTHER LIFE

I always liked to see and do different things, meet new people, talk to strangers, and listen to their stories. I always tried to leave the sameness behind. So, one part of me loved the idea of changing everything again, but when I thought about Aline, our sweet kisses hidden from her parents, and my dear friends, moving away, this time, was the last thing I wanted.

My frustration and conflict were depressing, and worse, useless. The decision did not depend on my will. My father maybe understood my annoyance, however, it wouldn't change anything. We would have to move once again. I knew it wasn't the first time, and it wouldn't be the last either.

So, I did not get to talk to Dad about it. He was not very available to talk, and when he was, wouldn't say much. He worked from very early in the morning to very late at night. It was hard to see him home. My school hours and his work kept us "apart". Breakfast was the only moment we were all together, but no one would say a word to contest his decision to move. Especially me, the youngest.

The moment of moving was approaching and the excitement of having new experiences was losing badly to the big losses that I was about to endure. Who would be my new friends? How would the new school uniform be like? (I always thought they were all horrible), but the worst thing that gave me butterflies in stomach, really bad ones, was to leave behind my Aline. I was terrified at the thought of the first BYE. Believe me, it was traumatic. I thought I would die. Maybe I would never like another girl the way I liked her: AALLLIINNE, the most beautiful name in the world! I decided that it would be the name of my future daughter, as far as I could keep a secret of why I chose this name and never explain my reasons to her mother. Can you imagine if she decided that our son would be called Braulio, the name of her first boyfriend?

Our farewell was very sad, but sweet, a mixture of melancholy and syrup. We hugged each other and cried. But what appeared to be a permanent pain and insuperable loss, soon went away, when I first stepped into the new house.

It was a great surprise. The first things I saw were a huge swimming pool, a big soccer field and a kennel. Everything a boy could desire in life. Don't get me wrong. I still missed Aline, sure, but soon, even she became just a good memory from the past. My mind now was completely crazy about enjoying the present: long pool baths, play soccer all day long in my own backyard and have a puppy. SUPER! I was already happy again. After all, I was only a boy.

A few weeks later, my brother and I got a dog called Belly, a white and brown beagle with black, beautiful little details. The only problem was that it was not very intelligent, had poor learning abilities and bed memory. It never learned the proper place to poop. So, playing ball in the soccer field was like being in a mine field.

Speaking of doing things, I remembered, my brother and I had a lot of household chores: cleaning the pool and the yard, picking up Belly's poop, doing the dishes, and helping out in the sewing workshop. I had not mentioned this detail before, but in this house, there was a large ballroom, which had become my stepmother's workplace.

Thanks to God my brother Fábio and I, were very close and we shared all the tasks. One helped the other to finish everything as quickly as possible. It was not because we were very dedicated, but because we could not start playing before finishing all of our obligations, including homework. My stepmother would inspect our jobs and demand perfection or do it all again. She justified her attitude saying that doing our tasks well would teach us to be better men in the future.

The problem was that if we finished our tasks too early (in her opinion) she would come up with few more... Children suffer!

She loved sending us every day to the pharmacy, supermarket, or any other place to buy something. Those places were two, three, four or more blocks away from home. I never understood why she couldn't give us a list (and a shopping cart) to buy everything at once.

At first, we were upset and very tired. However, over some time, we got faster and even ran. Our bodies became stronger, and we developed resistance. The strategy of going shopping in a hurry had two reasons: gaining more time to stay on the street enjoying the freedom or talking to someone before returning home and increase our ability to ran - good skill to play soccer and, who knows, in the future, compete in marathons. (Well, the marathon did not work for us).

Since we could not change our situation, we learned to change the way to face our reality and take advantage of it. A good lesson for life.

As soon as we were free to our duties, we would run in the neighborhood calling friends to play soccer, fly kites and play marbles at our home.

Nowadays only soccer remains popular in a kid's life in Brazil. Kite and marbles, nobody even hears about them anymore. The cities are bigger, the traffic, intense, and all kinds of risks and violence became a concern. Playing on the streets is not a choice. Thanks, GOD, for the video games.

But it was a good thing I enjoyed my youth very well. It was great jokingly playing pike, picks, glue and hiding games, hopscotch and together we all played mixed salad. For those that have never heard about it, mixed salad is when with your eyes closed you pick someone in the group and chooses without seeing, to hug, shake hands or accept a thong kiss. After soccer, that was the best part of the day. We also used to play "spin", where boys and girls are seated in circle and spin a bottle. When the bottle stop, the person in front of the end of the bottle must ask the one in front of the bottle mouth, "pear, grape, apple or mixed salad?" The answer was followed by action: Pear meant a handshake; apple was worth a hug, grape a peck on the cheek. But we all just wanted mixed salad, when the other side was a beautiful girl, who would have to accept a mouth kiss. OHH GOOD TIMES!

Nowadays is hard to see kids playing like that, maybe they invented better games. I don't believe it, but who knows? Have you ever played truth or dare? Very indiscreet and very dangerous ... very delightful!!!

One day Belly ran away. We spent days looking for it everywhere and asking everyone, but no one had seen it. It disappeared by magic. Maybe It already knew what was coming: My karma: friends, popularity, chores, routines, and CHANGES. Again, I've heard my parents talking about moving. AFF! Will it one day be different, and we will be in one home for a lot of years? I could not imagine any house that would be better than that one. Soon the family moved again.

BUT WHY NOT?
CHANGES ARE PART OF LIFE!

This time the change was less traumatic. I had no girlfriend to say goodbye to, and surprisingly the new house was even better than the one I thought was unbeatable.

The new house was a little smaller and had only a small pool and no soccer field. However, there was a huge backyard with all kinds of plants and trees, fruits trees. That house was so fantastic that I barely remember the school. A dream coming true.

The pool was tiny, but in return was much easier to clean. This aspect was good. HA HA HA! There was no soccer field to clean and collect dog poop. Great.

But not everything was perfect. As we entered the house, next to the gate, there was a mini and cute little house we thought it was a doghouse. As we were still shaken by Belly's disappearance and had not even thought of another dog, we decided to demolish the little "doghouse."

Breaking things for me and my brother was really cool. At this age, boys break anything, just for the pleasure of destroying, beating, flexing muscles, and competing. The opportunity was all we wanted.

Each of us grabbed a sledgehammer with enormous excitement, and started hitting the house, which broke down more at every hit. Then came the big surprise. It wasn't a doghouse! The house was a place for offerings to the saints of some cult of black magic. Inside there was a dead black hen, few dishes with yellow manioc flour and a bottle of rum. A genuine feast! We were impressed and frightened, but we had to finish the demolition. Scared and praying incessantly, we destroyed everything. But, from that day on, strange things started happening.

My brother and I shared the same bedroom. So, I have a witness. Two days after the destruction of the "doghouse", at about midnight, we heard strange noises, footsteps, and whisperings. We also saw strange white, translucent bodies! Ghosts? Perhaps we destroyed their house and now they were there to hunt us? I do not know, but I was terrified. As embarrassing as it was for us, two big boys, we ran to Daddy's room. My father told us to go to bed and control ourselves. My stepmother started praying for the souls to go away. Every night, for about two weeks, the three of us repeated this ritual.

Maybe because we were in the mood for ghosts, I remembered a song that talked about an old woman living under the bed with her animals.

"At night, the mouse squeaked, the cat meowed,
the dog barked, the monkey jumped,
the pig rooted, the goat bleated,
the donkey snorted.
And the old lady said: oh my god it's all over…"

We didn't find any woman under our bad, but we saw one staring to us from our bedroom window.

At that time, my stepmother's sister's son came to live with us. He was older than me and my brother. He was the one my stepmother cared most. One night, we heard a lot of noise coming from the kitchen. We dashed to see what was going on. It was scary. My stepmother was screaming, praying, and fighting with no one that we could see. But her nephew, who was bigger and strong them us, suddenly, was thrown to the ground and hit his head on the corner of the freezer. He passed out on the floor in a puddle of blood. There was a lot of crying and despair. So, my father runs with him to the hospital where he was treated and got some stitches in his head.

Later, my stepmother told us she was fighting a soul that attacked my cousin and disappeared after he hit the floor.

The adventures in this new home did not stop there.

One day, we decided to play cowboy. I had a little Monarch bicycle, and the competition was that one of us (my brother and I) would ride the bike and the other had to stop it using an elastic band with metal hooks on the edges.

The deal was if the if the hook attached the bike, the rider had to stop immediately. But once, my extremely nice brother did not stop, and the hook broke and it came back with full force in my teeth. Look what happened:

Another time, we were both handling some gunpowder to create a special effect explosion with flare, like Indiana Jones. To demystify the idea that only my brother was mischievous, while he was at the stage preparing the mound and the gunpowder trail to make the effect safely, by accident, absent-minded, I swear, I lit one match and threw it. He burned three fingers. Crying, confusion, and we were caught up again. Hahaha...trouble kids! It led us to be grounded for a while. Curiosity and a huge need for adventure, I guess, I've not changed much...

Even scared to death, my brother and I still would play in the yard of our haunted house at nighttime. It was like watching a horror movie. Even terrified we had to watch it up to the end.

When we had a party at home, or many friends around, we invited them to play hide and seek in our backyard at night. Of course, before we started, we would tell them all the old and recent creepy ghost stories, so everyone would be as scared as we were.

The darkness was almost total, as the backyard was full of big fruit trees, shrubs, and a huge bamboo creek, illuminated just by the moonlight. Our fear was real and constant. No one had the courage to hide alone, but no one had the courage to decide not to play either. It was better to dump our pants out of the fear than being called a coward and mocked forever... It was the price to play. It was valuable. Nothing was better than remembering and telling the others about our scares, screams, faces and victories. True or not.

That house was so good that I no longer missed Aline, or all those little kisses. I almost forgot the first HI. We ate fruits every day taken straight from the trees. How wonderful was suck sugar cane picked right there and pilled with our teeth. Great times!

Do you remember when I spoke about boys' nature to break things? Well, most of them also like to do mischief things with defenseless animals. I am sorry, but I have not been an exception. I remember well the wall behind the sugar cane bush. It was a brick wall without plaster. So, my brother and I competed to see who would stone more lizards passing in the wall. How evil! We produced our own slings. Fortunately, we did not have a very good aim. If you look at the wall behind the reeds, you could add up hundreds of holes the size of marbles or little rocks. We were blessed they were hidden. If Dad saw all those holes, we would be screwed, grounded indefinitely.

Have you ever thought about it? Do household chores (as ever) and even more, clean the bathroom, a new function aggregated to the others as I grew a little bit, (that I hated!), and all other extras tasks my parents could think of to keep me busy and, yet had the energy and be ready to play in the street, all kind of games you could think of. Especially one, "*pau na lata* " (hit the can with a ball). I will explain that one.

That game was awesome! A large size can was placed in the middle of a circle guarded by me holding a bat.

Another boy, or girl, on the other side had the same thing. The objective was to knock down the opponents' can. Each side has four or five chances to hit the other team' can, using a bat to throw tennis balls. The bat was used also to defend one's can. We invented an original sport:" baseball bowling".

Playing Atari, a very old video game, wouldn't be enough, I liked to be outside. Being grounded for a day was like losing a week of fun. When we are children, everything happens very fast. If you do not arrive at the right time for the soccer game, someone else will take your place. Whenever you are back, will have to wait for someone to get hurt or grounded as well. And sometimes we would make those things happen, "accidentally", just to get our place back. (I know it was not good).

To be grounded, in a child's conception, is like being jailed. No child wants it! In my case it happened quite often. Was I too crazy? In my opinion, no. I was just super curious, wild, and clueless. I just wanted to experience almost everything!

One day, I, my brother Fábio and my sister went to Barramansa, a small city in Rio, as we always did every time we could. It was our chance to change our environment and get rid of household duties. Besides, we still had the benefit to meet with many children our age that lived in the condominium of buildings where the mother of my stepmother lived. (My step-grandmother).

On that day, while my sister was dating a guy from the neighborhood who was also called Paulo (isn't that name, beautiful?), my brother and I decided to take the opportunity to race in the parking lot. I've always been very fast and zigzagged between cars to escape the others. But one time I missed the gap and bumped my knee into a metal part of a parked car. (An old beetle). I could say I was run over by a parked car. So stupid! The Beetle lowest edge was right at the height of my knee and the hit was tremendous. I did a flip in the air, worthy of a Hollywood scene, and I fell headfirst into the ground. A mess! To shorten the story, I've gotten ten stiches right at my knee, and also ruined my older sister's plans with her date. That story was over, but mine wasn't even close to the end. Besides the recovering time I also got grounded.

I still remember another interesting event that occurred when we lived in that haunted house.

Two blocks from our house, lived two beautiful twin girls about fifteen or sixteen years old. Nowadays, I do not know if they were as beautiful as a thought, but for me, at that age, any girl a little older than me with a nice body was considered beautiful. The problem was that I saw them as possible girlfriends, but they saw me as a baby boy. They were my cousin Thiago's friends.

What happened was that one of them, that I cannot remember which one (but it would not matter, because they were identical), liked my brother, who was very shy and completely unaware that the girl was flirting with him.

One day, she asked Thiago to help her to arrange an opportunity to kiss my brother. A true kiss, not those innocent pop kisses I used to exchange with Aline. It worked out. Thiago invited her to our place, and we were all together where once were the demolished "soul house". After a little while, Thiago told me we should leave them alone for a few moments. She was fast. Unexpectedly, she "grabbed" my brother and kissed him. When I saw what was happening, from my hidden spot of observation, I felt a little jealous, but not for long.

He tried his best to kiss her back, but he did not know how to kiss yet. Instead of using the tongue as everyone knows how, he was putting his tongue in and out, repeatedly. It made her laugh and later she told the details to my cousin, who told to someone, who told to someone else and so on, until they began to call him "little-tong" (In Portuguese, linguinha.)

I have to wonder if his shameful failure had something to do with the awkward location of his first kiss - over the remaining of the "creep soul house..." It could never be good!

Since we are remembering the first kisses, mine happened sometime later. However, I had not forgotten the lesson (thanks brother). The tongue smoothly extended in the right direction at the right time. Intensely, but calm. But now, thinking twice, I may have exceeded the intensity a little bit. If she was a little bit smaller, I think I would have swallowed her. I was lucky she never complained, and we repeated it several times. I think the main idea, for both of us, was to practice. Today, thinking about those kisses, I realized how bad I used to kiss.

I always loved kissing and at that time I was totally dependent on it. Perhaps mouth kissing is addictive? I once read in a book that a good kiss burns fat. So, one of mine could accelerate the heart, cause the temperature to rise, gives warmth and sweating. The girl may possibly lose weight. Makes sense! To kiss me is tasty and also medicinal.

Everything was going well in life, but time was passing and the differences between me and my brother seemed to be growing. How come? He was just one year and eight months older than me.

When we were kids the differences were minimal, even though he always had a stronger body than mine. But in the teenage years, the differences multiplied. We fought every other day, and also the days in between. The main reason was he had no time to play with his younger brother anymore because he was dating a girl who lived down the street. Her name was Rejane and she was his best friend's sister. A blonde pretty girl with bad hair.

One day we decided to fight when Dad was home. It was a very bad mistake. He was a man of few words, quiet and relaxed to the extreme, but that day he became an animal and for the first, and last time of course, lay his hand on us. He slammed us hard, and we got grounded for a month. No more dating or playing outside. After that, my brother and I were days without talking.

The only place we were allowed to go was my stepmother's sister, Teresa, on the weekends. She was very sweet and had a daughter, about my age, who attended the Christian Apostolic church. Then I made the choice to serve the lord and joined the teenager group of the church.

For some time, on the weekends, I used to go to Teresa's home and church, and my brother to dance parties. After a while I decided to join my brother and his friends. I always loved dancing.

The dancing especially with Brazilian funk music, was very fun. At that time the most popular dance was "the bottle mouth". Girls and boys had to dance squatting down until they got close to the mouth of a bottle placed in the center of the room. I became a professional. I was really good, a show on the dance floor. The girls would scream excitedly! Go Centipede! Go Centipede! Seemed like I was boneless.

At that time my sister, who is seven years older than me and lived in the United States, chosen to vacation in Brazil and visit us.

She came with an American boyfriend and decided to take us to spend the weekend with them in Petropolis, an historic city located at a mountainous region of Rio de Janeiro and built to be the vacation house of the Brazilian Emperor in 1845.

At the height of tourist season, there were no vacancies in any affordable hotel, and we ended up staying at the Motel Glamour. I must explain that in Brazil motels are meant mostly for sex purposes. The first problem was convincing the manager to rent a room to two teenagers.

It was against the motel regulations. The second problem was the two of us in a Motel room. Bizarre!

We were very curious. What would we find in the room? An inflatable doll? No. Champagne? Not even close.

We found a sex chair. In our complete ignorance we thought that it was an exercises machine. Immediately, we began an inspection to see how the chair worked. That's when we found the instructions manual. The drawings were only comparable to the Kamasutra! We were not totally wrong. It would take a lot of exercise to use the chair properly.

We didn't have the courage to ask my sister if she found an "exercising chair" in her room.

The next day we all went back home and too soon my sister was flying back to the US with her boyfriend.

Life was back to normal, all the same as ever! Including the situation my brother and I dreaded the most. We were about to move again.

AGAIN?

Fábio, poor kid, was going to lose his girlfriend and we would never see our very familiar ghosts again. We would miss them and also the fruits and the darkness in the backyard. We were sad, actually, disappointed.

But then, my curiosity took over. It could be good. Every time we moved in the past our new home has been better. However, I could not imagine any house better than the one we were living in. Maybe this time we would live near the beach or in a treehouse?

By this time, Dad started driving a new car. A Del Rey. Leather seats, air conditioning, power everywhere… super! Back in the days, those things were not common, especially in Brazil. It was a top-of-the-line car. Not bad. Maybe the new house would be fantastic.

What a disappointment! The new house was more like a jail. It was big, but it had steel bars in every window and two gates of pure and solid iron at the entrance. Perhaps it had been a jail before? Hahaha… just kidding!

Our backyard was reduced to a small front yard full of plants and flowers, only good for the bees, ants, and toads. Play there was beyond unthinkable, it was impossible!

Our housework also increased. The new tasks were to wash, almost every day, all tiled areas of the house:

porch, laundry room, garage, and everything around. To cope with the aggravation, the solution was having fun. We used a lot of soap to slide on the floor and dance rock and roll with brooms and mops.

I think my stepmother thought we were having too much fun and decided to add two new tasks to our routine to improve our education: wash and iron our own clothes. Life was more like an intensive housekeeping course.

The good things about this new house was that, for the first time in my life, I had my own bedroom and Tiago was no longer living with us. However, I was mistaken. It did not last long. Soon, to my great surprise, his sister came to live with us.

Even disappointed, I understood the situation. She was so pregnant, her belly was so big, that she needed a whole room to fit in. My desire to have my own room was once again postponed. It was ok. She needed some privacy. Pregnancy is the most beautiful stage of a girl's life.

Life was changing. Fábio and I were no longer in the same school. He went to the Regency, for his first year of high school. I was at Passaredo for my last year in middle school. I hated that name that had to do with birds and that's why it seemed like it was a school for little children.

I was only there for a year, but it was the school I liked most to go to because I could go there by myself.

In this school, I became friends with a blond girl called Juliana, from my classroom. She had pout lips, so cute and a little different. I have never seen a mouth like that in anyone else. She lived right near my house, and she was my walk mate to school every day. It was really nice! My brother, who had completely recovered from that former kiss harassment, was dating her sister's best friend.

It so happened that I needed to finish the assignment of our study group and decided that I would go to Juliana's house on the weekend to discuss our options. Once there, I clapped at the gate to call her. I was dressed in a t-shirt, shorts, and flip flops. While waiting for someone to answer me, I was reviewing my part of the assignment and the plans I had made to share with her. When I heard the noise of the gate, I lifted my head in a gesture a little too blunt and got a pleasant surprise.

I expect to see my classmate, a blonde, relatively tall for a girl with a special pout lip. But there was somebody else. She was the vision of my life. She was Juliana's cousin. She had dark skin, straight black hair, and large eyes, she looked like an Indian and her name was Aline.

Suddenly it was all happening again. I could not see or hear anything. She must have said hello, because if it was a HI I would have heard. After a moment of total inability to react I managed to say: - Hello! My name is Paulo, Is Juliana home? And before she left to call my friend, I wanted to confirm and hesitating a bit, but I asked: - What did you say your name was again?

When she said Aline, my heart jumped So I reached her hand and brought hers closer until my lips finally touched it. It was the first time I kissed somebody's hand while introducing myself. I felt like a gentleman in the 1800's. Good style. She was surprised and smiled, and it was all I needed. She then went to tell my friend that I had arrived. So, Juliana came, and she disappeared. What a frustration!

I worked with Juliana on our school project the best I could. But I have to admit, I couldn't concentrate! I was only thinking of Aline. I was glad that I had carried out some research on the topic the day before. Otherwise, she would have to do everything herself.

I do not know if it was the kiss on the hand or the strength of my thoughts, but the truth is that from that day on, Juju (short for Juliana) and I had two more companions walking to and from school: Mariana, my friend's sister, and my Aline (which was yet not mine).

My new Aline was a year and a half older than me. And was in the fifth grade. It was complicated. In school back then, she would be called "an angel eater" and endure a lot of bullying if our colleagues knew that something was happening between us. But I was determined to go for it, even though I did not know what to do, when or how.

I think I had a little help from my friend Juju.

Surreptitiously, of course.

One day, going home after classes Juliana and her sister started to walk a little faster leaving me and Aline behind. I knew that they were probably talking about us because every now and then they would look back with malicious smiles.

I had to do something. When we passed in front of a theater close to their house, I managed to get us totally out of their sight, calling Aline to the side of the building with the excuse of seeing what plays were showing.

Surprisingly, she accepted my invitation without hesitation or questions. Once we were protected against curious eyes and a possible audience, we got closer and, in a serene and simple movement, we kissed. Filled with anxiety and excitement, I can't remember feeling or hearing anything else. Time stopped.

My mouth trembled just by looking at her lips, so we kissed every day coming back from school and when I could go to her house in the evening. The good thing was that her cousins helped a lot, providing alibis if and when they were needed. I confess I could go without having to explain anything to her father. A frightening man.

I was devastated when she moved away from there. It was the end. Buá Buá Buá! I lost again! This time the second love of my life, but it was not that bad after all.

I used to spend almost every weekend at my aunt's house and had a lot of friends that were living close to her house. Besides, I was always having fun and making new friends at school and in the neighborhood. Everything was fine and many things happened very quickly.

Out of those many friends, some stood out and we ended up forming a quartet: Myself, Leandro, Eliezer (Fula) and Marcio (Maínho). Together we always went out to visit different places, especially churches, far or close, small, or big. Beside any other possible motivation, there were always many girls in churches.

This quartet was not of singers or actors. Our strong talent was the ability to keep an interesting conversation and our main goal was having fun and finding girls. We built strong bonds on trust of a real friendship.

On one of these visits to a distant little church, I met another Aline, (it's already a number 3), she was the pastor's daughter. She probably wasn't the right girl, but certainly she had the right name. I couldn't resist! It might be meant to be, and I would not ignore it. Besides, she was extremely beautiful and cute. We started dating immediately. I realized it wasn't a brilliant idea when the pastor called me to talk and asked many questions about my professional vocation and desires. So, it did not last much. We stopped dating faster than we started.

The quartet was not only successful in the city of Rio de Janeiro. At least one weekend of almost every month, we traveled to Conceição de Jacareí in Mainho's car, a Marajó twelve years old. If his car was not available, we would use the Mercedes transportation, called bus, with fifty-two seats. Conceição de Jacareí. is a small city close to Rio de Janeiro where the beach and the mountain are really together. The beach wasn't the greatest, but at the mountain, we could enjoy many waterfalls. The water was freezing but we did not care, it was fun!

The city had only one main street, a white sand beach with no waves, a very good bakery, a convenience store, and a little church. Few families actually lived there and were responsible for a lot of unformal jobs: renting equipment for snorkeling, selling coconuts, clothes, fast food, beach toys, hats, and everything else the locals and tourists needed or desired. There was only one place the tourists could stay for a few days. A little Inn with only six bedrooms that could fit, sometimes, more than sixty people. Only three restrooms. Nobody would stay there for comfort.

It was worth the two or more hours car drive and few miles walking to bathe in these most attractive waterfalls laced in the middle of the mountain, there were three of them, called: the Slide, the fun one; the Veil of the bride, the most beautiful, and the enchanted Draw-well, from where one could enjoy the most beautiful view of the mountains and the city.

The fun in the water, the scenic beauty, and a lot of flirting with the girls were paradise for the boys of Rio de Janeiro. Whenever we got there, the news of our arrival spread, and the local girls ran to the beach being received with applause and smiles. We were very successful with them.

Of course, there were other guys there, some locals, that we saw as constant threats, especially one nicknamed Merman. As soon as we heard about him, considering his nickname, we thought him to be fragile and sensitive, harmless. Once we saw him, strong and hairy, he appeared to us to be a sea monster.

Our quartet had to stick together the whole time, just to feel safe.

With our fame for being the kids from the city of Rio de Janeiro, we kissed a lot. All the girls wanted a little bit of us. In no time we became special, creative, and also very selective. Among us, we classified the girls. The chubby ones we called "mangrobas", (the mix of mango and soursop fruits), the ones with beautiful bodies, but ugly faces, we called "bugalús", (something like a chewed gum face). And the worst ones, those types that we can't describe without crying, we called "Jacamongas". I can't say no more!

I remember a real "jacamonga" that fell in love with my friend Leandro. She had a really strange, hoarse voice and very short hair. She was a nice girl, but Leandro was not as brave a warrior as our friend Tiago, who was never part of the quartet just because of his weird taste for girls. He could go for anyone. He was very democratic.

The quartet's routine on Saturdays and Sundays were sacred: We would meet friends at church to play and some worship and, if we were close to home, go straight to the Mauinho's aunt ice cream shop. On the coldest days, we were served hot dogs.

One afternoon, walking back home with Leandro, we went through a couple of girls talking. As we passed, they started whispering and laughing maliciously. We decided to come back and talk to them. This attitude was just my style. In Brazil, who acted like that was called a "wood face" meaning not shy at all.

I don't even know why, but this time, I chose the blonde and Leandro, the brunette, both against our preferences. Looking back, I understand that it couldn't have been different. Could you guess the name of the blondie? Yeah, you guessed right! It was Aline, yeah, the fourth Aline. A girl called Aline simply attracted me!

However, the name was not the only reason for my choice. The brunette was fine, but her eyes seemed to pop out, like a face in cartoons. She should wear sunglasses.

I introduced myself to the cute blondie saying looking deeply inside her beautiful eyes: My name is Paulo, but you can call me Paulinho as my close friends call me. She understood well what I meant and said smiling "I like Paulinho". I do not need to say much more. We started dating right there.

The return home on weekends after church and the ice cream place started to be more interesting and time consuming. I was the happiest boy, almost fifteen years old boy on earth. I wished it would last forever. I was in love, again. Unfortunately, it didn't last much longer. A few weeks after Aline started going to church with me, we broke up. I think it was due to my popularity with other girls. I guess it wasn't meant to be. I was feeling a little disappointed and running out of places to find someone new.

Around that time, out trips to Conceição de Jacareí started to occur less often. Well, the place did not have much to offer any more! There were no more girls available that hadn't been kissed by one of the quartet members. Let me explain. There was the understanding, whether spoken or not ,that friends shouldn't kiss a girl that was already kissed by another friend. Kid's serious deal!

However, a few weeks after the frustration with Aline we decided to return to Conceição de Jacareí and give it a try. Who knows if the situation was already different? It worked. I met a girl named Carolzinha. She was nice and beautiful, but she had a little problem. She walked like a duck. Can you picture it? But the real problem was that I thought she was too small, too tiny, and young. She was only thirteen years old, and I was fifteen and tall for my age. I felt uncomfortable. It seemed I was dating a child. We stopped dating almost as soon as we started.

It was a good decision because soon after I met my fifth Aline, right there in Conceição de Jacareí That name haunted me. The positive thing about only dating girls named Aline was that if I misspoke and called the girl I was, with the name of an ex-girlfriend, she would never know I was thinking of another girl.

We went out only a couple times. It didn't work out. We lived too far away from each other. Besides, at that time I became interested in dating older girls, with more experience. However, the older girls, seventeen up, were very difficult to catch, especially for me, the youngest of the group. In general, they were looking for older boys, with money and nice cars, but I'm not a man to give up before try really hard. For my positive attitude I was well compensated.

One night, at a little bit wild beach party, while sipping a fruit popsicle, I saw her. A brunette with a great body, beautiful dark skin, the blackest perfect curly long hair, deep black eyes, and a wonderful mouth. Suddenly, I could be in love again. Her name was Fernanda.

I do not know if she was interested in younger guys or maybe just curious to know the taste of a boy from Rio de Janeiro. It didn't matter. I was lucky! We dated for a few weekends. But one day, when we arrived in Conceição de Jacareí I was told she was seeing someone else, older than her, that also lived there. I expected that to happen one day, but not so soon. I have no regrets.

After that, Conceição de Jacareí was no longer attractive to me. There were no more challenges or new adventures. So, we went there a few more times and our trips finally ended.

I wasn't aware, but my dad's firm was not going very well. One night, he told us that my brother and I would be going to a to a new school. Instead of a private school we loved, but a public school not very close to our home. It was a shock. We have heard terrible things about public schools in general. Violence, drugs, bad food, and lack of good teachers. But we had no way to avoid the new reality. We were terrified.

Believe it or not, things turned out not so bad. To start, I liked one of the major changes, the dress code. We went from wearing an ugly uniform to wearing jeans pants (good to hide my bird legs), any shirt of my choice and an ID (my first).

Soon I started playing soccer with the guys at the new school Because I was a good player, soon I was very popular, made a lot of new friends and realized the teachers and all the people working in the school were nice. The new school was not like what people had said at all.

It was nice that me and my brother Fábio were in the same school. It helped me to increase the number of friends I had. I knew everyone in the seventh and eighth grades and a lot of students from the lower grades too.

I was very popular by then and I decided to use it to bring some improvement for our school, running for president of the student's association. I wasn't sure I would be elected, but I was! It was very cool.

One of the things I did as a president was organizing interschools sports championships: handball, soccer, volleyball, and ping-pong. Of course, I've participated in all of them, but the ping-pong tournament was the one I won. I was very good back then. I also organized chess games and other smart games for the nerds, and a fashion show to please the girls. The purpose of all those activities was to have fun, but also to gather food and money for a few poor communities. Many of those schools' students came from poor communities.

The first fashion show was an event to be remembered. The group of models who participated was not selected by their beautiful faces, nice bodies, or popularity. We stimulated anyone to try it.

The result was that we had representants of all types: too tall, too skinny, too rounded, and some really hot girls and boys.

The board of five judges and the present crowd had the huge responsibility to elect a Girl and a Boy "Henrique de Magalhães" (name of our school).

The winning boy was my brother. I bet his success was due to his strong legs. The girls loved them. They were just like my father's. I never understood why my legs were so thin. After all, like them, I also played soccer.

Well, maybe God does not give it all to one person! I was, by far, a much better talker and more outgoing person than them.

It was around that time, the end of seventh grade, that I met an eighth-grade girl named Aline, during a school trip to the countryside of the city. The trip was nothing special. I don't even remember where we went and what we did. I'm mentioning it because of two things. First, I decided to forget about going after girls named Aline. Finally, I understood that the name Aline had nothing to do with beauty and charm. The Aline on this trip was the opposite of all expectations that her name could bring to my mind. She was shy, lanky, and a little corny. A disappointment. The second reason was a felt it was time to explore other names.

The girl of the moment was Isabel. I contacted her around lunchtime, halfway through this field trip. Although I will always have a spot in my memory for Aline number one, Isabel was the most beautiful girl I had ever seen or dated. I couldn't believe that for the first time, I was falling for a girl with a different name.

It was not because I was still mulling over the disappointment with Aline number six that I refused to go with my friends to the swimming pool after lunch. The point was that I wasn't in the mood to show my athletic little frog body to everyone. So, I decided to stay quiet on a recliner by the pool, trying to write some poetry as I always loved to do since I was a little kid. I was also having fun watching my friends going crazy in the pool. Observations and records could one day be useful. We never know. It was when I saw her. She was wearing a green shorts and a green bikini top.

She had straight brown hair, up to her shoulders. She was simply walking, but for me it was like she was parading in slow motion! I thought I saw her glance at me discreetly and then sat down, displaying all her beauty two recliners ahead, wearing nice sunglasses.

I had to get her attention! I reached for my little notepad, and suddenly touched by an inspiration I wrote:

If I had the ocean, I would want just a drop; if I had the entire sky, I would want just a star; and maybe, if I had everyone in the world, it wouldn't be enough if you were not there.

Then, driven by some strange and strong force, I went up to her. At that moment I did not notice if I walked fast or slowly and couldn't even tell if she was looking at me or not. I just sat on the recliner right next to her. I was quiet for a couple seconds because I couldn't think of anything interesting to say. You know, a bad line can ruin all the good intentions and chances.

Finally, I said smiling "Why are you here alone?"

I heard her say something but could not even register in my head what she had said. I was daydreaming, looking at her adorable mouth and extraordinary body. I had no idea what she answered.

I was surprised when she turned to face me, took off her sunglasses, and said: "Did you hear what I just said?"

I did not know what to say. If I said no, she would think I wasn't paying attention to her and get mad. If I answered yes, I would be at risk because I couldn't respond to what I barely heard and didn't understand. On top of that, I did not want to start a possible relationship with her on a lying mode.

So, I apologized and said: "I did not hear a thing you said because I was distracted thinking about what I had just written for you." It was a perfect strategy to make her curious. It worked, just as I wanted!

She moved her legs very sensually. I guess I will never know if it was natural or on purpose to tempt me. As I expected she asked: "What was you writing?

It was my chance to lead. I answered: "Nothing important, just a few things to keep memories of, until the moment I saw you, when I stopped immediately and wrote something different, straight from my heart."

From there on she was extremely curious. She insisted on knowing what I wrote, but I did not say anything. Perfect! Now I had the knife and the cheese in my hands! I had to act quickly and intelligently to keep her interested.

It was time to call her for a walk around the farm. I was sure she would accept it. Certainly not for my looks (actually I wasn't very attractive) but because girls can't stand not knowing a secret, especially when it is about them.

I was totally focused on her; at that point I couldn't see or hear anyone around us. I only cared about two things: do not talking nonsense stuff, and do not trip, because I couldn't take my eyes off her.

Perhaps she was my first third love? Or my third first love? It didn't matter.

When eventually I came back from the wonder world, I realized that we were really alone. Talking distractedly, we walked far away from everything and everyone. We ended up on the top of a small green hill with a magnificent view. Then, we kissed. A kiss that almost made the day into night. Amazing! But maybe it was because time had flown. It was already time to go back to the farmhouse. The night was coming fast, and we did not notice it. Something really special was happening.

Instead of a pop kiss and running away as the first time I stole a kiss, this time the kiss was not stolen but we had to run anyway, hoping to catch the bus before it left us behind. We made it. Actually, the driver was waiting for us for about five minutes already.

Of course, we could not escape the avalanche of nonsense jokes from our classmates. I think being popular helped a lot at that moment because even though we were late, we still found two empty seats, one next to the other, to travel back home together. Love was totally in the air.

This time, I didn't even think about going to the back of the bus where I usually traveled in fieldtrips. I wanted to stay right in the middle, away from the teachers sitting in the front, and far enough from the bustle coming from the last seats. In the middle was perfect and neutral, because as the song says, "I just want to kiss, kiss, kiss ..."

From that trip on, "Alines" never again. Isabel was my new and real love now. She was perfect! Like me, she was very popular. She was part of a "belly dance" group that performed in events and parties. Of course, I was always with her.

Unfortunately, nothing is always perfect. Her little brother was always with us. I had no choice. It was that way or no dates with her.

The only moments alone would only happen when we faked school assignments at a friend's house. We did that a couple of times.

I could not be happier. That fieldtrip changed my life. For the first time I was dating for real. I wanted to go over to her house to talk to her parents and all.

One day, I just did it! I met the whole family. My terrifying father-in-law was actually a short, funny, fat guy, with a huge mustache, and a joker, just like me. I loved him! Her mother, who answered to the terrifying name of mother-in-law, was a young woman, very pretty and super friendly.

Because of her, I even thought that all mother-in-law stories friends had told me before, were lies. But she was totally an exception. Wait until you know my future motherin-law.

Isabel had only one annoying problem, a nine-year-old brother. He was chubby and had an Indian hair style, straight and heavy. He looked like a mini-Franciscan priest with a real vocation to be a third wheel.

He accompanied us everywhere; I could not even be alone with her at her house gate. I wanted to die of chickenpox because of it! But I had to live with it to be with her. Trust me, she was totally worth it. Even having to put up with her annoying little brother, I was happy. Really happy!

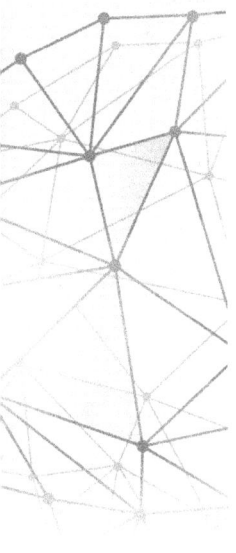

CHAPTER II

An Unexpected Journey

When everything was going very well in my life, one afternoon, surprisingly, my father called my brother and I for a very serious conversation. Talking to Dad was a rare thing and we were worried, anticipating that something bad was about to happen. Would we go to another house again?

We were about to learn that it was not a conversation at all. It was a plain communication that our lives would undergo a radical turn.

Without any preamble he said:

"In ten days, you both are going to live in the United States with your older brother, your sister and your birth mother".

At one time, we were going to leave behind not only our house, but also our city, our country, our stepmother, that I knew as my mother since I was three years old. And worse, all of our friends and girlfriends.

I was desperate, angry, crazy and all other word you can think of! Why was this happening? Why at this moment? I was just 15 years old, but I was exactly where I wanted to be. I couldn't accept losing everything I'd worked so hard to conquer. I was about to finish 8th grade; I was the president of the students' association of my school; And I also had the prettiest and finest girl in the neighborhood - Isabel. I was living my best days. I couldn't believe this was happening to me!

But I had no choice. I had to pack up.

All of it was very drastic and dramatic, but it wasn't even the worse thing. Even knowing that my real mother lived in the United States, I had never wanted to learn English. I used to study French. One of my dreams was one day grab a backpack and go to France. Never to the United States.

From that day on, it felt like we were in a marathon. With kisses and tears we had to say so many goodbyes to classmates, family, and friends from almost every church I've visited. It was horrible. I was really sad, but not as depressing as I felt saying goodbye to Isabel. Unthinkable. I was sick and tired of being abruptly forced to end another chapter in my life and start everything over once again.

Of all the things in the world that I couldn't understand was how the word never and forever could be so close to each other. At that moment, I was feeling so many bad emotions that I couldn't even think about the possibility that out of this chaos could born something good.

Finally, the time had come. The plane started moving and the flight attendant announced: "Fasten your seat belts, we will take off, Have a great trip."

It was my second trip to the USA, but the first one without a date to return anytime soon, or perhaps ever again.

The first time I went to the USA was a couple of years before. We spent a month at my sister's house in North Miami Beach.

At that time, we all visited Disney World: my brother Fábio, me, my sister, and my real mom. It was a dream coming true. We were so excited and anxious that we left home very early to get there as soon as possible. When we arrived, our car was the only one in the parking lot. The problem was we didn't bother to write down where we parked.

We spent the whole day enjoying as much as possible of everything in the park. We got in every line; we saw almost everything. We did not want to miss anything. Some attractions were super cool, others just interesting. The rollercoasters were the best. I loved them all.

At the end of the day, we were exhausted from walking the whole day. Once we got to the parking lot dying to seat at our car and leave, we looked desolate at the sea of cars in front of us. Where was our car?

We sadly realized we had only two options: sit on the ground and wait until all the cars left or, go looking for it. We decided on the second option. Each one of us started searching in a different row. Once in while one of us would shout "I found It"! We would all run towards the call only to find out it wasn't the right car. How many golden Grand AMs could be there? Hundreds?

After one hour or so, we felt defeated. Luckily, a security guard passed by in a golf cart. He kindly offered to help, and my mom went with him to look for her car. About a half hour later we were back on the road.

On that vacation my mom offered to teach me and my brother how to drive. Of course, we said yes.

Besides the Grand Am, she had a navy-blue pickup truck that was a little older than the Grand Am - our training vehicle. The street she lived on was a dead end and we drove up and down it many times for about a week or so. She was our instructor.

I was doing well. So well that she asked me if I was ready to drive the truck backwards into our grassed backyard. I wanted to show off and I said I could do it easily, with no problem whatsoever. I seemed so confident that she believed me.

Well, the task was not as easy as I thought it would be. The open gate was big enough and the yard was huge, but right in the middle of the lot there was a big tree. It was so big that three large men interlocking hands, couldn't embrace it. Just passing the tree was a big wooden kiosk used as a birdhouse.

I did not hit the tree, but my first-time parking backwards was a disaster. I went right into the kiosk. The thing was exactly like the Tower of Pisa in Italy. I like to think that even though it was an awful mistake, I did what I was supposed to do. I set all those poor birds free.

At the time of that trip, I believed it was only a normal vacation. But now, I'm sure the excuse to visit Disney, the dream of almost every child, was preparation for what was being decided about my future without my consent and happened nearly two years later.

Everything happened in no time. Suddenly I heard the voice of the flight attendant. It was for real! The plane wasn't even off the ground and my heart was already dying from homesickness. I almost yelled! "Stop the bus, I'm going down!" Oops, plane… But I said nothing, it wouldn't matter anyway! The plane took off, and there was nothing I could do about it. My best option was to relax. It was a night flight, so I settled in as best I could, since I was in an economy class seat.

It wasn't that bad because I was very tired from all the emotions and stress and slept for about seven hours straight. When I woke up, breakfast was being served.

However, I needed more than food. Maybe I needed a chiropractor or a can opener to get me out of that extremely small and uncomfortable seat where I was stuck for so long.

There was still about an hour to go before landing. Time enough to use the bathroom and appreciate the view of the city below that grew bigger and bigger by each minute.

We finally arrived in Miami, Florida. Maybe because I was a little older, two years after the first visit, or maybe because I knew I would be living in this city forever, my senses were very sharp.

First, I notice the organization of the airport. Everything were clean and functional, and the employees were polite and helpful. But it wasn't all. The people coming and going were also nice, neat, perfumed and educated. Even those passengers who, like me, had just been rescued from the plane seats after a night of torture. Now I could understand why such an urgency to use the bathrooms! Looking good was a priority. No one should expose others to the smell of sweat, disheveled hair, and dark circles under the eyes.

I mentally compared the airport to the bus station where I used to catch the bus to Conceição de Jacareí. What a difference! Men and women, children and teenagers selling everything: candies, ice cream, hats, tickets to the soccer game, marijuana, and other items, as well as beggars of all ages, races, and strategies.

Against my will I began to think that maybe not everything would be as bad as I thought, after all. Somehow, in the back of my mind I knew that all the things and people I had left in Rio de Janeiro would always be there. I just had to find the way to go back there one day.

My sister was waiting for us at the airport. She was happy. Kissing us she said: "I'm sure you both wants to go home, you must be tired, hungry and curious."

Immediately, I realized that my home was now somewhere I didn't even know. I felt weird. I didn't want to upset her, but I could not let her comment pass in blank. Quickly, I said: Ok, let's go to your home. I felt I needed to let her know that I wasn't feeling so happy. She just smiled.

The next step was to get to her car. Where would it be? We followed her for what felt like forever. I had forgotten how big this airport was. Some people would need a GPS. When we reached that enormous parking lot, I've expressed my worry if the experience we had two years ago leaving Disney, would happen again. Laughing, she showed me the ticket. I relaxed and directed my attention to the cars parked in there. Some, I had only seen in Hollywood movies: gorgeous and extremely expensive.

Finally, we reached my sister's car. it was a red Honda Civic, hatch back with tint glasses, all "hooked up". By this time, I was already excited to leave the airport and see more.

My first surprise was that I didn't see any mountains. That was weird. They disappeared or when I was in Miami two years before I didn't even notice it? I was also surprised by how wide the roads were and next to them there were no bakeries, little soccer fields or sidewalks full of people. A certainly a change.

I wandered how could I live without a fresh French bread in the morning and afternoon and no soccer games in the neighborhood.

My new house was a two stores home in a condominium of about two hundreds other houses very similar to each other. It was not new, but very nice and comfortable: three good sized bedrooms, a huge living room and a backyard not very large but enough for a barbecue grill and a swimming pool.

The house was close to a supermarket, where I started my first attempts with the new idiom. It was actually, very funny.

Every day I gathered up courage, took the little shopping list, trained the pronunciation of each item, practiced how to ask a few questions, and went.

My first attempts were based on phonetics. As I listened to Mom speak, I repeated and just to be sure I pointed to the item in my list. People trying to help me would give me instructions, by saying, for example: "Go straight three aisles down, turn left and it will be on the third shelf on your righthand side ". Did you understand? I would say anything to them but thank you. So, they all believed I did. Thanks to God usually they pointed the direction I should go. At least it was a start. It was no piece of cake.

The supermarket was huge, at least three times the size of the ones I used to do my shopping in Brazil. Sometimes I had to ask the same question again and again (to the cutest girls, of course) to find one item. Can you calculate how long it would take me to buy ten items? Thankfully, I was able to find a few things just by looking around. Amazing how American lettuce and chicken looked just alike the ones in Brazil.

It looked like a boring little life was beginning. The memories of everything I left in Rio de Janeiro started to bother me a lot. I had no friends to be with, no places to go.

Nor even school to go to. It was vacation time and I had nothing to do. On top of that, watching TV felt like I was watching a silent movie. I could not understand a word.

One night, my mom came home from work with great news. She asked if we would like to go to the 15th birthday party of one of her Brazilian clients' daughters. It sounded like a miracle. My brother and I responded immediately. "Of course, anything is better than staying home doing nothing."

The party was in the ballroom of the condominium where her client lived, really far away from our house.

Over the weekend, we went out to buy new clothes for the party: We bought beg pants, polo shirts and new sneakers. Everything was cool!

We arrived at the party a little late. The hall was already crowded. All the girls were wearing long fancy dresses, and every boy was wearing a penguin suit, or tux. We stopped at the door with a cruel doubt. Should we stay or should we go?

At that point, everyone had already seen us. So, we decided to wear a poker face of real professional players from Rio de Janeiro. We entered the party carelessly, showing a lot of confidence. All eyes turned to us. We knew nobody, not even the birthday girl! As we were already ashamed, we must as well make it worthy.

Later we understood why we went to that party wearing the wrong clothing. My mother was living here, in the USA, for time enough to know about the sweet sixteen style party. She only forgot that, in Brazil, that celebration happens when the girls were fifteen years old.

Little by little, the party was getting boring as hell, no one was dancing, and it seemed more like a funeral. After two hours surviving in the party, we decided to do something about it. So, we asked the birthday girl if she would get authorization to play a Brazilian CD of a new samba group, the most successful in Rio de Janeiro, that we had in our car.

Even hearing the new CD everyone stayed just as they were before, seated, and bored! I couldn't resist it any longer. I got up from my chair and pulled my brother into the middle of the room and side by side, we started dancing on the empty dance floor as if no one was watching us, but all eyes were.

Thanks to God, soon enough all the guys were with no coats and no shoes, and the girls, when possible, had folded up their long dresses turning them into miniskirts. It was amazing and good for the eyes. We were successful. Soon, everyone was thanking us for rocking the party. Gladly toward the end it all worked out fine.

I wonder if mom did it on purpose, anticipating that the boys from Rio would make the difference. I have my doubts. She wouldn't be that bad! Would she?

Unfortunately, every teenager at that party lived too far away from us. Because of that, it was difficult to keep in touch with our new friends and life went back to the boring routine we hated, but not for long. Soon enough Mom came out with something new.

Although excited, we were also kind of worried. What would it be this time? She explained: "A client of mine just arrived from Rio de Janeiro with his family: wife and two teenage daughters, Paula, and Frances. Are you guys interested in meeting them? Immediately we decided to take any possible risk. Why not? It ended up being great. Excellent.

Paula, was my age and their parents used to call her Paulinha (little Paula). It was exactly the female version of my name Paulinho (little Paulo). I was quickly enchanted with her. I don't know if it was because of her pretty name, or her beautiful pair of legs and other nice body features. But probably, it was because of her big smile and beautiful green eyes. Really charming. I wasted no time.

Strange. I traveled to another country to date a girl who could have been my neighbor in Rio de Janeiro. I was happy again.

By then, I was sixteen and already driving. Sometimes, we went out at night, always with her young sister to hold back our young and crazy desires. A couple of times we got home very late and her parents, already my friends, invited me to sleep over. I loved it because I had the chance to sleep in the room with the girls.

I'm sure her parents thought I would sleep quietly in the camping bed on the floor between the two girls' beds. However, her sister had become our accomplice. Instead of reporting the little things she heard and saw to her parents, she covered for us. The reality was that as soon as we heard their parents' bedroom door close, I climbed into Paulinha's bed, or she came down to the camping bed to be with me.

We've learned a lot about each other's bodies during those nights. If her dad ever found out, we would be in big trouble. He was a huge guy!

Before the summer was gone and school started, we were always together. It's easy to explain. I didn't have any other friends and the same could be said about the girls. We just had each other. It went that way for a while. We were happy and I was in love, anyway. But when I started being popular at school, she got really jealous for no reason. I didn't tolerate it well. Even though I've dated a lot of girls, I've never cheated. It would be repugnant. Besides, I hated her attempts to control me. I always loved to make friends. So, our relationship ended, but we remained good friends.

At school, I quickly discovered that I didn't need to speak a good English to make friends in South Florida. There were fifteen Brazilians in school and to communicate with others, I used *Spanglish*, *Portuglês* or *Portunhol*. Words designated to express a mix of Portuguese, Spanish and English, the idioms I knew or was learning. And there was always a chance to use gestures and body language.

When the classes started, I was very worried. In other words, I was terrified. I left Brazil in the middle of the eighth year and here I would go to the 8th grade. The problem was that I didn't speak any English to understand the classes. Thanks to God the school had English as Second Language (ESL), a special program to foreign languages speakers.

The first day in the ESL class felt like I was in the Tower of Babel. The one in the Bible where no one could understand each other because everyone spoke a different language.

There where thirty students like my brother and I. They came from all over the world. Some were from different countries of South America, such as Chile, Argentina, Peru and Bolívia. Others, come from Europe – France, Italia, Portugal, and other countries, or continents like Asia. I met Chinese, Vietnamese and Koreans. We were all in the same boat. We were trying to learn English.

We were not the only Brazilians in that class. There was also a girl named Maria Clara, who was shy, tiny and a little chubby with gorgeous green eyes hidden behind thick glasses. She was a lovable girl!

We got together in a group with the South Americans, Spanish speakers. It was easier to communicate with them. Portuguese and Spanish are very similar. Interestingly, we could understand almost everything they said, but they did not understand us. I also could say a few words in French, especially to the girls. I would love to do the same in Chinese, but it was impossible and still is. It's a shame the oriental girls are so cute!

ESL class was only the first class of each day. The other classes were in English. Can you imagine the difficult it was for us to participate in classes such as history or science?

I was more relaxed, and I even enjoyed the math classes. First of all, the numbers were the same as in Portuguese. However, because I couldn't understand what the teacher was explaining, I had to see the examples to have an idea about what was going on. I felt very luck when I perceived my teacher was teaching something I had already learned in Brazil early in the year. My classmates thought I was a genius! Helping them all was also very good for me. It expanded my network.

Everything, in the first day at school was a challenge, beginning with finding my brother among all those kids during the break time. Since we did not know where to go or what to do, we followed the crown that led us to the cafeteria. From that day on, pizza and sodas were our everyday options. Once in a while, we would add a salad, just to impress a girl and start a "health" conversation.

Thankfully, the school was huge, and we had to go for a long walk from one class to the next, which helped us to burn the extra calories we ingested. This, and the fact that the gym class was right after the break.

At first, I delayed in starting to do each exercise. The gym teacher looked at me strangely, until he realized that my problem wasn't the exercises, I just did not understand what he was asking us to do. So, I had to wait to see what my colleagues were doing and do the same as them. That teacher was nice. He even tried to explain the exercises and rules in Spanish. It helped very little. He spoke too fast in Spanish.

One day I've got to know that I needed to choose at least two elective classes. Anything from plants to astronomy. My first option was Spanish. It would be nice to speak three languages. Of course, after I learned English and Spanish. Besides there were a lot of Spanish speakers in the school. After all, we were in South Florida.

My second elective class was sculpture. I had two reasons for this choice: first, I always appreciate all kinds of art. Second, I knew I was terrible drawing and painting.

The first contact with the clay, soft and cold, made me fall in love at first touch!

I was taken by Michelangelo's spirit, I think. The class began badly. The first instruction was to put the idea on paper. I could not do that. I had no talent to draw. I would never come up with anything closed to what l imagined. I had to do something if I wanted to be in this class. So, I started to manipulate the clay trying not to let the teacher see what I was doing.

My first job was a piggy bank with spiked hair, an earring, sunglasses, and a surfboard on its back. It was my first time sculpting something. The teacher was speechless. So, she said that I had art in me, and that I did not need to draw if I didn't want to.

From that day on, I was very creative. I did a lot of other cool sculptures, including a speedboat and a cigarette smoking fish, full of details, which also wore sunglasses. Although I thought I was a pretty good sculptor, I was still only a beginner and making eyes on sculptures was too difficult.

The smoking fish and a little research on the environment protection, and sea pollution got me to win the first place in the district school science fair.

My art teacher loved my work so much that I've never got any grade less than A+. I was the only student given clay to take home because I said I wanted to do something bigger, and I would not have enough time in class.

Actually, I caused an impact on my teacher and classmates when I took my masterpiece of art to class. It was a woman's body naked with all the nice details including a well-trimmed pubic hair. It had no head, no arms, no legs.

Ms. Britton, my teacher, did not know whether to applaud or yell at me. The class was in total shock. It seemed like no one knew how to react. But the shock was immediately followed by laughs, and funny comments.

Of course, I got another A+. I loved that class. I wanted to be there for as long I could. I still have that woman.

Unlike Brazil, the good thing of studying in Florida was that since the beginning, the students know what classes were required to graduate. What happened to me was that I came to USA in the middle of the year, and I was going to the 8Th grade in Brazil However, I did not finish it. The school year in Brazil starts in February and finishes in December, So, I was enrolled in the 8th grade again. So, I lost half a year. My desire was to anticipate classes to go faster to High school. So, I decided to implement a strategy.

Since I was very advanced in math because I had seen in the 6th grade, the subjects there were studying at that moment in the math class, I asked my teacher if I could go to the math final tests.

Before agreeing with me and let me do the tests, she decided to challenge me. She said I would have only a week to study and one hour to finish forty questions. In case I failed, I could not miss any of her classes because she would deduct five points from my grades for each absence. Besides, to finish with my arrogance, I should collect bubblegum from under the tables in the cafeteria for a week in case of failing the test.

I think she was only playing with my mind. Those threats couldn't be real. Nevertheless, I felt butterflies on my belly. But I could not back off. I was confident about my knowledge. I accept the deal.

On the day of the test, somebody left me in a white room, very cold and completely silent. I was tense, nervously sweating and had to deal with an annoying bug in my head that was trying to push me down. I had to be strong. In my mind I saw my success and said aloud: "I will make it."

The teacher applying the test asked me to show my hands, arms, and legs. Maybe I was hiding some useful information in my underwear? Well, nobody wouldn't know, but back then, I didn't even wear underwear.

In no time, I heard someone asking if I was done. I quickly checked sheet by sheet and answered. "Just a second, my name is missing."

My body was also done. I suddenly felt very tired. I left the room, but my mind didn't. I couldn't think of anything else. Even if I wanted, my friends wouldn't let me forget it. In all possible idioms, they were teasing me, anticipating my penitence. Some friends offered to lend me some plastic boots, to help me in cleaning the restrooms, others brought me a little knife, and nicknamed me as boogers remover. They all believed I was going to fail.

For a week, I was mentally "tortured" by doubts and fear. Finally, I received the results. Halleluiah! I've succeeded. Now it was my time to mock my friends. They were all going to math classes, and I was going to a very pleasant new elective class, weightlifting, to put my body in shape. Soon, I achieved my goal, a six pack.

By then, I already knew some English, but I didn't practice much because all my friends were Brazilians or Latinos, Spanish speakers. The only American friend I had dreamed of being Brazilian too, just to have that way with the girls that made as famous at school.

On Halloween of this year, maybe 1999, the family decided to go to Coconut Grove to have fun. We invited a few friends. We were fifteen of us in total, including my mom, dressed as teenagers from the 50's with ponytails and a backpack. We all had to use costumes, but we didn't choose vampires, witches, or those alike.

My sister was very cute dressed as Cat Woman; her boyfriend was a Viking warrior. I have no idea why he chose this costume. That hat with horns was horrible... My point is that in Brazil, getting horns means your woman is cheating on you in secret.

All the boys went wild. We were all dressed as drag queens. My brother Fábio was a ridiculous cheerleader, with those strong and hairy legs. Markus, my best friend at this time, and I were nurses, the boosties you've ever seen. On me, it really looked like a costume. Even though I had curly long hair, I also had a goatee. Markus, however, didn't have any hair on his face. He actually looked like a girl.

Until reaching the parking lot of the party venue, the countless cars had to go very slowly. Our game was to approach the nearest cars and show our hairy legs, offering companion services and pressing our fake boobies on the window. What a night!

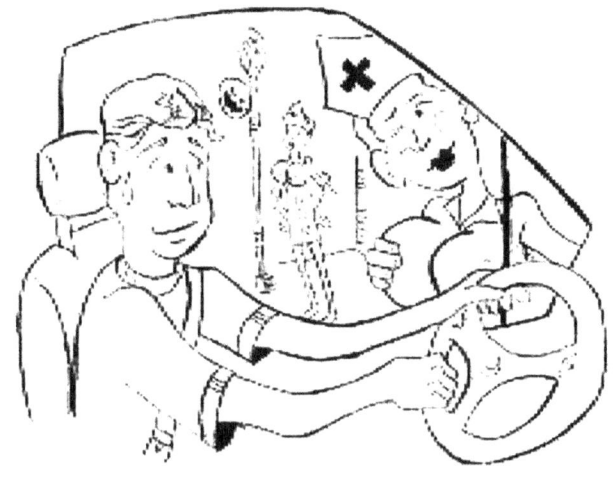

Being home during school breaks was not boring and bad anymore. We could watch TV, play soccer with our friends, or play with the new puppies, Rusty, and Freckles. They were cute little Dalmatians, that André, my oldest brother, brought home when he visited us that spring. He and his wife were the owners of the house, but they were living in New York for a while.

I loved that house and the dogs. Freckles was always quiet and lazy. Eventually, we discovered he had a kidney problem. Poor dog!

In contrast, Rusty looked like a child. My brother trained him to catch the tennis balls we threw. He was very good at it. He Jumped and grabbed the ball in the air and run to bring it back to us. But there was a problem. He wanted to play nonstop. He would bark incessantly until we threw the ball again.

Sometimes, to rest our arms, we would throw the ball in the swimming pool. The break wouldn't last long. In a few minutes the ball reached the opposite edge of the pool and Rusty was already there to grab it and come to us to re-start the game.

My brother and I were already well adapted to our new life. However, we were missing some extra money in addition to our weekly allowance, to spend on parties and girls. So, we decided to get a job.

Once again, our mom intervened. She introduced us to another one of her clients. He had a fiberglass boat mini factory. He needed some extra hands to finish two new boats.

Working on the boats was not an easy job! We had to learn how to apply resin with an iron roll and sand everything. Sanding the boats was worst of all. Fiberglass dust flew and fell on us. We were constantly itching. We could wear overalls to protect ourselves, but the heat was intense, and we preferred to wear short-sleeved shirts.

Although the work was hard, it paid well. Something around US $8.50 per hour. More than the minimum average wage for our age and experience, which was around US $5.00 per hour, at the time. We were very happy.

We worked hard to learn English, make, and save money. It compensated. In a little over a year, we bought our first car. It was a red used, but not too old, Pathfinder. It fit five people comfortably, but most of the time we carried ten or eleven. It was awesome.

Everyone talking loudly, at the same time, singing funny Brazilian music and laughing.

One of our regular destinations was a night club. But we had a little problem! No one of us was twenty-one yet. So, the solution was simple. We had no choice but change our birthdates on our old Brazilian's IDs. It was not difficult. the Brazilian's ID were not a real card. It was a simple plasticized paper. At the night club entrance, we would present our fake Brazilian's IDs, say we were tourists and none of us spoke good English. It always worked. We usually went to night clubs on Fridays or Saturdays. Sundays only if it was a special event or a new girl was not available before.

The following day, it would be hard to go to school. We were all very sleepy. But we never missed it. After all, you know, for boys, more important than do crazy things, is definitely to tell the stories to their classmates. Not everything, of course. Some things can't be said.

My tendence to date older girls has intensified rapidly in that period. Mostly because, in the clubs, everyone thought that I was at least twenty-one years old. I enjoyed meeting cute girls. I didn't mind their age. I just wanted to have fun. I even flirted with girls almost around my mom's age at that time, late thirties.

Only once it went very weird. I started flirting with a young woman, very attractive, around late twenties, so I figured. A few moments later, a girl about my real age, hugged her from the back and smiling asked: 'Mon, who is this guy?" I got really embarrassed. The girl was even more interesting than her mother, but I couldn't change gears. Minutes later, I disappeared.

Always, when the music stopped and the club was about to close, we would look for a twenty-four-hours restaurant for breakfast. Sometimes after dropping off all my friends, I had to go straight to school. Those restaurants were not very good. However, the alternative would be even worse, the school breakfast. When there were no school the next morning, some of us would go to the beach to enjoy the moonset and the sunrise.

By that time, I was not dating, and I felt free as a bird. Then something happened.

Markus, do you remember him from the Halloween party? The one who wore the same nurse costume as mine? He was almost my next-door neighbor. He lived in the same condominium on the street behind my house, and we went to the same school. He lived here in the US since he was a baby.

So, when my brother and I arrived, we became good friends. He greatly helped me to adapt to the culture and continued doing so throughout our friendship. We used to play beach volleyball and he was also part of the Pathfinder crew.

One day Markus showed up at my home with the most beautiful girl ever! I thought he was bringing a friend to introduce to me. I felt very lucky, but he said: "This is my girlfriend, Millie". What a disappointment! At that moment I started to have an internal and very uncomfortable conflict. I thought his girlfriend was the most beautiful girl in the world! All the Alines, Isabel, Paulinha, every one of my former girlfriends had been immediately forgotten when I saw Millie. But she was the girlfriend of my closest friend. I could not and I would not do anything. So, I decided, more or less, to get her out of my head, but I also decided I should stick around. This way, I could preserve my friendship with Markus and start a new one with Millie.

Later on, I became their confidant. I heard everything from both sides.

Markus told me he was tired of her because she didn't want to have sex with him. What could I say? I had already thought of that with her too! What a shame…! I told him to relax and respect her will. Sex would happen at the right time if it was meant to be, without any pressure.

Around the same time, Millie complained to me that Markus only thought about sex, asking me what she should do.

Full of demagoguery, I answered: "It is natural at this age, hormones, and discoveries… to which she replied: "I know, but I don't feel ready yet.

I decided to invest my time in a little investigation, asking her how long they had been together, what she really felt for him, and if she loved him. I think she answered all my questions, but I have not heard a thing, only imagining what would be like to kiss her mouth! It was happening again, way stronger than ever before.

When she stopped talking, I knew she expected me to say something. I simply said: Do what your heart is telling you to do. What else could I say?

A couple of days later I heard they had broken up. Being Markus's confidant, I had to listen to his outburst: "_ I got tired of trying… I gave up."

Millie also came to me, crying. I felt pity for her sorrow ,and her tears broke my heart, but I confess. I wasn't sad at all. My opportunity had come.

However, I was still best friends with Markus, and I had never before dated a friend's ex- girlfriend. I was not comfortable with that situation. Nevertheless, I started talking to Millie every day at school, and also by phone. I wanted to see her smiling again. If Markus noticed it, I couldn't tell. We wouldn't talk about it, at least not yet. We didn't want to lose our friendship.

But it was hard to disguise. Every time I saw Millie, I felt the chills, and every hair of my body stood up.

Help eventually came from whom I least expected! Markus, himself. One day he called me aside and said: "I think that Millie is into you. Go for it, I'm with another girl already." He was only thinking, but I've been sure for a long time already. It was worth waiting for the right time. It came! It was now time to change my status with Millie.

The opportunity did not take long to happen. At the end of the following week, with the whole group, including Markus and Millie, we went to the beach. On the way back, I dropped everyone off, as usual, including Markus, and no one lived closer to me than him. Finally, it was only Millie left in the car with me. It was all premeditated, I took her home last.

When I stopped the car to drop her off, I ran around to open her door, and also help her out, like a real gentleman.

I followed her into the entrance hall of the building, and it was time to give a goodbye kiss. As usual, I grabbed her hand to kiss it. Maybe I'm the last man in earth to kiss hands. I did it, but not only that! I pulled her close to give her a kiss on the cheek. Actually, three kisses to get married, (it's a Brazilian thing). But when I got closer to her cheek, I suddenly switched the three usual kisses for just one in the mouth. Calm, lovely and hot, very hot. And that was it, just the kiss, no words needed!

On my way back home, I had to stop for an ice cream to cool down. But I ended up drinking only a glass of water. I did not want to replace the taste of that kiss with any flavor in the world. I didn't even want to brush my teeth that night , but don't worry, I did. I was a very lucky man!

That is how our love story began. We saw each other every day. We couldn't get tired of it. Actually, we definitely wanted more time together. But it was hard to manage because I had to study and work. Our time was very limited. If we could go out at night after my work, things would have been different, wonderful.

Unfortunately, nothing is perfect in life. There was a mother -in-law. My nightmare. Well, we were not married, but I wished we would be in the future, and there is nothing worse than an Argentinian mother-in-law. I had to put up with her because Millie was worth every sacrifice.

After nearly two years dating, I started to understand what Markus was talking about. It didn't matter how in love we were, nothing sexual was happening. Her mother did not give us any chance. We were never alone, and Millie never went with me to parties or nightclubs. The closest thing to private moments was when we went to the cinema to watch PG-13 movies with her little sister.

Millie did not try to stop me from going out at night, but I did not feel good about that. I wanted to be free and feel no remorse, but still enjoy life. However, I wanted her to be part of my life. The problem was her impossibility to come with me wherever I go due to her mother's restrictions. So, every now and then I broke up with her despite all the love I felt for her. As they say, we can't have it all.

Our times apart were always short. A month or two was enough time to feel that she was sorely missed. The nostalgia returned. Our love was elastic. As the saying goes: "the real man is not the one who conquers several women, but that one who conquest the same woman several times." I think I was doing it! Though, I was twisting, a little bit, the meaning of the saying.

Every time we were apart, anything could happen. Date other girls, travel, hang out with friends. I just enjoyed my youth and energy.

One day, my elder sister, who was six months pregnant, decided to change her car. She went from a Cabrio convertible to a family car. Her big belly couldn't fit in a sport car anymore. It was also not safe to drive with a baby on it. I was lucky! I sold the pathfinder and assumed the payments on the red convertible.

I was in heaven. I had long hair, three bright earrings, my body was finally in good shape, and I was driving a convertible car. I was living the best days of my life!

Our group of friends was still together, but Marcelo and I started to get closer. He was a couple months younger than me, but also a couple inches taller and stronger. He was a jiu-jitsu fighter. When I was not with Millie, I was spending time with him.

Once we met two girls in a nightclub, Tara, an Italian. Her name says it all, doesn't it? And Catherine, a girl from northern Europe. They were both very beautiful. Tara was a brunette with straight hair, medium height, and a perfect little body. Catherine looked like a mirage. She was tall with red hair and light green eyes. Marcelo and I were very excited with them and planning a long night. However, like Cinderella, they told us they had to get home before midnight. What a disappointment. We left them at home and did the usual, we went to Denny's to eat something. They had our phone numbers and swore they would call us. We knew it would happen, but when?

We had not even finished eating when my phone rang. Surprised, I said Hello, what's up? They were already calling us. Catherine's sensual voice said: "Helloooo, Pauloooo, can you guys come over?" "Of course, I said, but what about your parents?" She said: "no problem, they are sleeping. When you get here, do not knock on the front door, take the side path. The bedroom light will be lit and the window open". We could not believe what we were hearing. We left Denny's restaurant immediately.

When we arrived there, we kind of panicked. There were two windows half open with the lights on. Maybe her parents fell asleep while reading and forgot to turn off the lights. We knew that one of them was Catherine's father's room. The only solution was to call them.

Climbing the window was the easy part. We did not waste any time. As we entered Catherine's house, Marcelo went to the bathroom with Tara and, I luckily stayed in bed.

We enjoyed our company all night long, and before we knew it was already morning. We had to get out as fast as possible. We started to get scared when we heard noises that sounded like someone was approaching the girl's room. We panicked. Her father was at least twice our size, horizontally and vertically. We jumped out the window and ran without looking back. That was close! A few minutes later, she called me saying that her father had just entered her room to say good morning.

When I was with Catherine, I was always in some danger. Once, we couldn't resist the cozy atmosphere of the elevator of Marcelo's condo club house.

It was a shame when Marcelo had to return to Brazil. I had to do all those crazy things alone. Well, what could I do? But, by that time, I was already addicted to jumping in and out Catherine's window.

My energetic lifestyle and the risky nights were amazing, but I was already missing Millie a lot! So, I had to give up all the action and fun I used to have with Catherine and Tara and try to regain the one I loved.

This time, even dating Millie, I no longer felt remorse in going out with friends to night clubs. I thought it was a way to preserve our relationship. She totally agreed with it, and even encouraged me to do it.

Without making too many sacrifices, maybe I did not need to ask for a break again!

One more, unfortunately, it did not work out. One night at a club, while I was having fun and dancing excitedly, I noticed a brunette flirting with me. At first, I pretended not to see it. I did not want to see it! But she continued dancing sensually and teasing me with her eyes.

She had light brown skin, muscular thighs, a well-made thin waist, and nice breasts. Pretending I was a full not understanding what was happening, I got out of the dance floor, and I went to the bar to drink a Coke. I needed to get away from temptation. But she was at the bar too. I introduced myself, and right there, she pulled me out to dance saying she was also Brazilian, from the state of Bahia. Her name was Mirella.

The night was passing, and we were talking and dancing. We danced a lot! I used to love dancing! The night was almost over, and we didn't even notice it. When it was time to say goodbye, I reached to give her a kiss on the cheek. It was when I heard an extremely loud sound. A *boom* from the band speakers. I got startled and I missed her cheek and hit her mouth. What a sin! However, as if nothing had happened , we exchanged phone numbers and said goodbye.

I spent the night and the whole next day thinking about Millie. I felt worse than the bandit's horse poop. A total piece of shit. I was feeling horrible. It was a sunny Sunday and instead of going to the beach, I went straight to Millie's house. I was downtrodden and disappointed with myself. I had failed to be faithful. I really needed to talk to her.

When she saw me with my eyes full of tears, she asked me what had happened. She was worried, of course. Asking lots of questions: "Are your parents OK? Is there anything wrong with your brother? And so on… I was speechless hearing her concerns and worries. It made me feel even worse. I did not know how to tell her, but I couldn't hide what I've done!

So, I took a deep breath and told her everything at once. I talked so fast that she could barely understand what I said. "Forgive me, unintentionally, but wanting to, I don't know, I kissed another girl. I need some time. I'm confused, and I think I don't deserve you!

She stood like a statue in front of me, without moving and without saying a word. I was so sorry, but the damage was already done! Then, crying too, she said: "Ok, let's be only friends"! What have I done? I knew she was the one I loved truly. I just wanted to enjoy life!

After that Mirelly and I met sometimes at nightclubs, parties, on the beach, all occasionally at first. It seemed like we were looking for each other! But now though, I was single, and she had also just broken up with her boyfriend to try to go with me.

When we started dating for real, we noticed that we both liked to dance, travel, and ride my motorcycle. I had not mentioned before that I had a motorcycle because Millie wouldn't ever ride it with me. So, every time I was with Millie, I would be driving, never riding. On the other hand, being with Mirella was always full of adventures. We used to ride my bike to go everywhere. I love motorcycles.

We traveled at least one weekend a month. We never went too far away, but we went everywhere-Key West, Key Largo, Tampa, Orlando, and many other places. We had our independent lives even while living with our parents.

Mirella was a professional Brazilian dancer and also played "capoeira, her body was fit and extremely flexible. For me it was almost a fantasy woman, all elastic. We could have sex anywhere: motorcycle, car, even in a bathroom of a bus, if we wanted it.

She also had a sister. But thankfully, she was older and had a boyfriend. That was very convenient, because he had a license to drive boats and the girl's stepfather had a nice sailboat. Once in a while, we went out on it. Whenever we were not sailing, we traveled on my bike. We did all we could not to stay home on weekends. We dated for a little more than eight months, but we ended up doing a lot more than Millie and I did in two years.

Now you must be thinking. What about Rio de Janeiro, my old life? Have I already forgotten the ones I loved there because of all of this excitement? If so, you're wrong. Dating, agitation, and travelling was not enough, believe me! I always remember everything I left in Rio, family, and many friends. I had a feeling everything would be on my mind for a lifetime.

So, one day, I decided that I had to go back to Brazil to visit all the places and people that I had left behind. So, I bought a ticket and flew to Rio de Janeiro.

When I got to Rio, things were exactly as I had imagined they would be when I left to USA, immutable. Everything and everybody were, still the same, only two years older, but I was different though. I had money in my pocket. At that time one dollar was about three Reais (Brazilian currency). What a blessing! I had taken a little more than a thousand dollars, which was equivalent to more than three thousand Reais. A lot of money to spend in only two weeks. A started renting a car. Next, I organized a beach barbecue to reunite all of my friends and traveled with the quartet to Conceição de Jacareí.

I enjoyed my fourteen days in Rio as a genuine tourist. Always with one or two friends, I visited the Pão de Açúcar (Sugar Loaf) A landmark with an extraordinary view of the city, the Corcovado (a huge statue of Christ on the top of a mountain), and I completed a track at the Tijuca Forest. All famous tourist attractions. I also went to the best-known beaches, such as Copacabana, Ipanema and Recreio dos Bandeirantes. Every night we enjoyed interesting restaurants and nightclubs.

It's unacceptable that I had to live in another country to get a chance to come back and get to know my own city. Being in Rio as a tourist was a blessing experience!

I also met Isabel, my lovely ex-girlfriend. She was even more beautiful, but nothing happened. She had a boyfriend and I still had Millie on my mind. In fact, I could not understand why. That was not right. She wasn't even my girlfriend anymore.

Right there I decided that whenever I got back home, I would end my relationship with Mirella and give up all the trips and parties just to get back to Millie. She was the one I loved and wanted to spend the rest of my days with. Even if I had to put up with her severe and controlling mother.

So, as soon as I landed in Florida, I began to think how I would change my life and get back to Millie. Ironically, I found out she was dating another guy who, by a twist of destiny, was Mirella's ex-boyfriend.

I got so mad! But I knew I only had to wait a little bit. Their relationship wouldn't last long. He would give up soon. I would have another chance. Millie and I were meant to be together. Our love was greater than anything. I just knew it.

I started doing what I had to do. I took Mirella's out for a nice dinner, worthy of an unforgettable relationship. After all, we were friends and adventures partners: the bike rides, camping tents, and a very spicy story. I explained everything to her, and our loving relationship ended right there. She understood and got over my decision faster than I thought. I was free and ready to get my love back. I had to be careful, very cautious, but fast. I had to move softly, nonchalantly, but assertive. I would not become her best friend. I had other intentions. Once best friends, forget it. Best friends will be forever.

In a courageous strategy, I came close to her mother, my ex-in-law! It wasn't bad at all!

One day, to my surprise, she told me she did not like Márcio to be her daughter's boyfriend, and that Millie would be better off with me. I wonder if she didn't like anyone who dated her daughter. So, she liked me better because I was the ex. Márcio was the target of the moment. What she didn't know was that I would be probably the next Millie's' boyfriend. How will she feel about it?

Poor Márcio! He was the ex of my recent ex-girlfriend - Mirella and the current boyfriend of my former ex - Millie. I was already making my move to change my status with Millie and make him the ex of my future girlfriend. What a mess!

Finally, I got what I wanted. I was back to Millie. He must hate me today, and maybe forever! Hahaha! Sorry about the laughing. It was mean!

Once I was dating Millie again, I was happier than ever. However, I had to adapt to the new situation. On the days I knew I could take her home I went to school driving my car. The rest of the time I just rode my bike, it was my passion. She was always telling me to sell it, but my answer was always the same and immediate:- never! I will one day be a super bike racer. My bike was a GXR 600 cc, beautiful and new.

As I dealt with the girls, sports and friends, things were changing around me, and I did not even notice it.

It was a surprise that my father, who was divorced from mom for almost fifteen years, was coming to live with her and with us again. Was it love, passion, longing for his children or just convenience? I'll never know. The important thing to me was that our family was going to be reunited again - father, mother, and four children, not kids anymore. The family was even growing. There were another family member. The daughter of my oldest brother, André. She was nearly one year old.

When my dad arrived and Andre's family returned from NY to live in Florida again, Mom, dad, Fábio and I moved into an apartment on the beach of Hollywood, Florida. Only my sister would be keeping on living there with André. The apartment at the beach was a temporary rental, until our own house, also in Hollywood, became unoccupied.

The building was not senior housing, but about seventy percent of the residents were over sixty years old. But the place was great and the location even better. On one side was the lagoon, and on the back, was the sea, the beach, and a nice pier, great for a date on a full moon night. It was just ideal for romance.

However, as nothing in completely perfect, the parking lot of the building was under construction, and we had to use a parking lot across the street. An open space protected only by a gate that opened with a magnetic card. I wasn't worried about leaving my motorcycle there. After all, I had good insurance and believed that robbery did not exist around there.

I guess I was wrong, one day I woke up, put on my leather jacket, grabbed my helmet, went down, and did not see my bike to ride to school. It was stolen! I got really mad!

Millie didn't even mask that she loved what had just happened to me. But I was devastated. But I was also relaxed because I knew that the insurance would give me another one in no time.

A week later I was riding a Kawasaki Ninja 750, and already planning my dream bike for the following month, a TL 1,000 Suzuki Yellow and black. I was hoping for someone to steal my bike again. I thought about gluing a tag on it that read: Could someone please take me home; don't you think I'm beautiful?

It would not have worked because shortly after, we got back to our house. which for a while was rented to my grandfather with his companion nearly forty years younger than him. Moreover, as his relationship didn't work for him, she left. We all moved in, also to help him to get over her. It would be very sad for him to live alone.

After some minor renovations, our house looked much better. It no longer had the huge bird's house, yeah, that one I crashed years ago, freeing the birds. Instead, we made a volleyball court or a soccer field, which we used as needed. We also got a trampoline. We still had some free space on the backyard for my nephew and niece' playground.

Next to the pool we put a Jacuzzi that accommodated up to eight people on the paper, but in reality, it would fit at least fifteen. (Just like my pathfinder).

There were also a foosball table, a bar and a billiard table. The ping pong table was portable. We put on the pool table when needed. The house looked like a club house, we had everything!

Grandpa and his dog Luna stayed with us. He was my instructor at the billiard game and lived in a separate suite next to the swimming pool.

My brother and I were very lucky. Our grandfather was almost deaf and refused to wear his hearing aid. He was never bothered by the noises my crew and I did.

My bedroom and my brothers were in the front of the house. We almost had an apartment for ourselves. Two bedrooms, a living room, and a bathroom. We could come in and go out as we pleased without being noticed. The rest of the house was the kitchen connected to the family room and a master bedroom which was my dream room because it had a huge closet with mirror doors that covered the entire wall. It also had a direct exit to the pool area.

The only problem was that my mom wasn't deaf at all, and some nights we had to keep quiet. Unthinkable, it was impossible! We were always in trouble. It was part of the game! Do what? No pain, no gain…

Christmas parties in this house were historical! The whole family, friends, guests, and freeloaders never failed to appear. At the last Christmas party at that house, my nephew and niece were already saying that they knew Santa Claus was my father.

They claimed they had never seen grandpa and Santa together. We did not have any excuse to deny it. We had to innovate! We put all the male guests in a box to draw out the name of the new Santa. Our intention was to cheat and make Nestor the winner.

He was a family friend who already carried a natural Santa's belly. Sadly, it did not work! Nestor's son, my friend Bernardo, was the one chosen to be Santa.

Bernardo was a great friend and accepted the challenge. Unfortunately, I do not think we did a good job transforming Bernardo into Santa Claus. We placed a huge pillow under hir shirt to make his belly as big as Santa's . The problem started when he bent down to get the first gift from the magic bag. His fake belly 'almost went up to his head, stopping super funny on his chest area, allowing him to be the first Santa Claus with big boobs instead of a big belly.

We were all dying to laugh, but we didn't until the kids looked at him with funny faces. I've never seen a Santa Claus so horrible! Actually, neither did any of the kids at that party.

At this time, everything in my life was wonderful. I had a nice job as a concierge in a fine hotel that paid me very well, and as always, many friends.

I was finishing high school and making thousands of plans about going to college in France, or somewhere in Europe, probably with my love if she wanted to. I often played volleyball on the beach or rode my motorcycle. I was the happiest man on earth. Better than I've ever been before. I've definitely found my place in this world!

TRAGEDY! THIS TIME THE CHANGE WAS FOR REAL!

One day some friends called me to play ball at a soccer field near the school. I accepted right away.

As Millie was not with me at that time, I rode the bike, but I left the helmet at home. After all, the use of it was optional in Florida.

The field was very close to my house and the day was very hot. The helmet also bothered me a lot because of the three earrings I used to wear. That is why I didn't wear my helmet sometimes.

When the game finished, I could think of only one thing! Get home, take a shower and be perfect to be with Millie again.

But the imponderable happened! In a fraction of a second, somehow, the motorcycle slipped on something, and I fell. While falling, I hit my head on a fire hydrant. It did its role very well and put out my fire for a long time.

With the lateral impact on the fire hydrant, I cracked my head almost from ear to ear, causing multiples damage in my brain. I also got a huge scratch on my leg. But that was nothing!

I was lucky. Just when the accident happened, a nurse from the local hospital saw me and immediately called 911.

Thanks to God, I was here in United States and the hospital was just two blocks away. I was told I got there in less than five minutes and ten minutes later I was on an operating table.

From the moment of the accident on, for a while, I could not remember a thing. So, my narratives about the following days after the accident, were memories that I created according to everything I was told later on. Except the vision I had when I was in a coma. I remember that I was entering heaven, but God told me: "You are not allowed to enter. For instants I became desperate: I died; I lost my love, and I'm also going to hell! I started arguing. Have I been that bad? Is it because I had sex before marriage? Or because I was not going to church every Sunday. But God continued:

"Be calm my son, it isn't your time yet. You have to go back and keep on living with my purpose for your life.'"

Uffa, what a relief! I had not died! It was a miracle of God. I always believed in miracles. I was even in love with a girl name Millie, short for Milagros (a Spanish word for miracle).

I was alive to have a chance to do what an old saying tells us. Every man, before he dies, must plant a tree, which I had already done, write a book, thank you for reading it, and have a kid, yet to come!

Everybody around me was saying that they were living a horror movie. The worst thing was that I was the protagonist of it. On the first and second days, more than 200 friends, colleagues, and some teachers came to visit me. Sadly, the news they received were not very encouraging. Doctors were talking about disconnecting the machines that were keeping me alive. I was not responding to any stimulation. No brain activity.

God knew better. It was not yet my time to leave. I was lucky again. When the doctors shift changed, a Colombian doctor decided to try one last resort. To drain my head, which at that time was almost like Minecraft cartoons, head, shoulder, and chest all the same size. I had to be sedated and kept in an induced coma. I couldn't take the enormous pain from my intracranial pressure that was 80mmHg, whereas a strong headache, a migraine, is somewhere between 5mm Hg and 15mmHg. If I wasn't in coma I would have died of pain.

Almost two months after the accident, I began to wake up. Millie was at the hospital. She would come almost every afternoon to be with me. She and my family were the only ones believing I could come back from the land of the dead. Actually, she was the one noticing my first small movement, a little tremor of one of my right-hand fingers. Before that, for a little while I could already hear people talking around me, but I was unable to show any kind of response.

At first, no one believed when Millie said, all excited, that I had moved my finger "- It's impossible! Or it is your imagination". Believing it or not, the doctors ran some more tests. I was really able to move one finger, just a little, when asked to do so, but nothing else.

From this day on, I started progressing very slowly, but promising, and sometimes embarrassing, when my little guy down there was up at full power. I was forgiven, as it was definitely not intentional at that time. Either way, it gave me some relief. At least it worked. What a shame if I was actually thinking about that at that time. I probably wasn't. But now it sounds funny.

The point is all I could do was move some fingers voluntarily. The rest of my body was a failure. I couldn't smell, I couldn't see properly, I couldn't speak, I couldn't balance my head, and I was eating through a tube in my belly. And the worse, I wore diapers. A total deterioration from head to toe.

To make the scenery even worse, I couldn't perceive what was real and what was fantasy. If it was not for a delicate moment like that, it would be comical that I believed that the chickens shown on TV, were under my hospital bed. The most scared moment was when I big Lyons came running toward me. My mother turn off the TV.

During the almost six months I spent in the hospital, I improved a lot! I could already recognize all my friends, remember facts of my past, and speak a little. However, my speech was very slow, my voice rough and my facial expression wouldn't change a bit. So, no one could tell if I was happy, mad, or sad.

On top of that my short-term memory didn't work at all. When a friend visiting me went out of my sight, I would forget immediately that they were just there a few seconds ago.

My physical appearance had also changed a lot. I went from athletic and fit to skin and bones, and from long curly hair to a bold head, full of scars.

Doctors' predictions that if I survived, I would be like a vegetable, incapable of doing anything, did not materialize. I was slowly getting better. Thanks to God! It was finally time to go home.

Upon returning home, I was pleasantly surprised. I finally got the best room in the house. The one I dreamed about in the past. That huge mirror was everything I ever wanted before. Unfortunately, at that moment, it no longer had much use. My image needed some upgrade. And I needed new plans.

Gaining weight was the first step. That wouldn't be very difficult. After six months eating by feeding tubes, I was craving the pleasure of eating real food. While being fed by tubes in the hospital, my brothers used to joke around saying "how is this rare filet? Did you like the chocolate cake? Want some more stroganoff? My brothers are good guys and funny. I would have done the same for them.

At home I would eat a lot of anything at my sight. For breakfast, a big bowl of oatmeal, a huge glass of a fruit smoothie with milk, and two ham and cheese sandwiches. A few hours later, in the middle of the morning, during my four hours of physiotherapy, I used to drink two glasses of chocolate milk. For lunch, I would eat anything enough to feed two people, followed by dessert, which was usually ice cream. A lot of it. I still had the afternoon snack. A bowl of fruit salad covered with condensed milk. At night, the menu was lighter, only a glass of Nesquik and a big chunk of Hawaiian bread with eggs or ham.

It was all part of my recovering treatment! So, in no time I've got back all my hotness, actually even *r* little more than I've planned. All of sudden, I was a little overweight.

My next plan was to relearn how to read and write. It was not an easy task. I didn't have good coordination of my eyes and my hands. It was like going back to kindergarten. Try to color large figures, cover dotted letters, read, and write known words, then small sentences and so on.

As the time passed by, out of so many friends I had before, only a few stayed close. Millie, Rodrigo, João and Thiago. My closest friends at the time of the accident, especially Thiago, who also had a motorcycle and was at the soccer game with me on the day of the accident. Rodrigo was a surprise since I had met him only a few weeks before the accident.

Thiago was from the northeast part of Brazil. He was a very good friend. But he was not selective when it came to women. He had no criteria for what he wanted in a girl. If anyone smiled at him, no matter if she was too skinny or fat, ugly or beautiful, he would go for it. Among our friends he was known as the warrior! In contrast to St. George, who killed dragons, he loved them. And was also called Picasso, but to explain that nickname in English would be impossible, just the Brazilians can understand this joke.

St. Thiago best disciple was our friend João, who learned the rules of war very quickly. He used to repeat "In love and war, anything goes." I have to disagree. Even though I had the accident that put me in a wheelchair, being selective has always been part of who I am.

After the accident, it took me a while to go back to school. All my time and effort was put into working on my rehabilitation. My life consisted of physical therapy, occupational therapy, speech therapy, hydrotherapy, and all other kinds of therapy you can think of. My routine was eating, exercising, and going to doctor's appointments. For a change, my parents, every day, took me for a walk early in the morning, to sunbathe and change the environment.

Millie, my sweet love, came to visit me every day. However, even enjoying her company pretty much I felt she was exhausted and under a lot of stress. She was starting college and had to work to pay tuition and all of her other needs. She was an adult now and had no more allowances. Then I realized that no matter how much we loved each other, everything was very different. My life could no longer be the same and neither could I. The accident had left deep marks not only on my body, but also on my mind. I knew that one day I would get better, but I didn't know how long it would take. We both know that none of us would have the courage to break apart. We loved each other very much.

One day she told me that she was going to turn down a scholarship offer in another state because she didn't want to be away from me. It was by far, the most beautiful proof of love I ever had from anyone in this world. Shakespeare, and all his poetry could never express the given love we shared.

Her words were beyond beautiful, but I could not allow that to happen. Against all my body's will, straight from my heart I said: "Millie, you cannot give up your opportunities to fulfill your dreams because of a friend". She replied immediately. - "But you are not just a friend, you are the love of my life!"

Even suffering more than words can describe, I knew that I had to set her free. She had the right and duty to be happy. To take advantage of all the chances in her life. I cared more about her than about myself. She was living her best days, young, beautiful, healthy, intelligent with great opportunities in front of her. At that moment I had nothing good to offer. It wouldn't be fair to put her through so much struggle and disappointment until that day came.

I cried like a newborn baby. So much that I almost dehydrated, but I did what had to be done. I loved this girl the way real love is supposed to be. For the first time I gave my true love the first last Kiss. I just wanted her to be happy, even if her happiness wasn't with me! This experience was terrible, almost the same thing as being bitten to death. However, by this time I've learned to be conscious and resilient. I only had to hold my head high and live my life as best I could.

I would still always go out with my true friends. It was a great group, a new quartet: Thiago, Rodrigo, João and me. I was blessed! We used to go to restaurants and walk on the sidewalk on the beaches. Well, they walked, and I rolled. It was healthy and also fun.

One night we decided to go to the movies. It was the first time after the accident that l was going to watch a movie at the theater. At that time, it was an adventure for me because doing even little things such as peeing was very difficult and time consuming. Peeing seated is easier only for girls. Wisely, I went to the restroom before the movie started, but it took me a while to do it, wash hands and try to zipper up my pants, unsuccessfully of course, but I got back to the room a little bit before the movie started. Everyone was already seated but the lights were still on.

A fiasco happened when I asked Rodrigo to help me transfer from my wheelchair to the seat of the theater. I wanted to be comfortable. However, my bad memory got me in trouble. I forgot that I failed to buckle up my pants. When he helped me to stand up, my pants fell down all the way and I was not wearing any underwear.

For everyone, but me, it was a comic presentation before the movie started. Rodrigo did not know what to do: laugh, hold me up, or help me to pull up my pants. He decided to laugh. What a bastard! Thanks to God, the lights went off.

RESTARTING

I was back at school about two years after the accident. If everything was easy and a piece of cake, before the accident, now it was all too hard and complicated!

My first problem was reading. It was really slow and I still had a very bad short-term memory, and even worse eyes coordination. Every time I got to the end of the line and tried to go to the next one, I always ended up reading the same line again and again because I couldn't remember that I had already read that line. To make things even worse, sometimes, my eyes sent me to two or three lines down. Therefore, is comprehensible I usually didn't understand what I was reading. It seemed to me that all I had to read was too complicated and confusing. I blamed the writers.

Over time I got better. I could read a paragraph and remember the previous one. What an improvement!

For a while writing was even worse. Maybe in another life, I was a German. I didn't know where to separate one word from the next. The result was a very long single word that finished when the line in the notebook ended. It was a good thing that the notebook was in the portrait format. Imagine if it was in the landscape!

However, it was a significant progress. In the first step in the process of relearning how to write, I could not perceive there were a space between the letters in a word. So, I wrote one letter over the other. It was hard to read it. Took me a lot of training covering dotted lines and following orientations from my mother and a speech therapist to see each word emerging.

Even though the letters were too far apart or too close to each other. My brain was all confused.

At school it all turned out not to be too hard to resolve. As in the past, all girls were willing to help me the whole time. They copied everything I needed and never let me forget what I had to do. The tests were a problem. Although I could use my notes and had extra time, it was really difficult to find what I needed in my notes. Sometimes I would even forget what I was looking for.

Going to the restroom was another adventure! I knew I couldn't miss one bit of any class, since it was already too hard to keep up and remember things. Therefore, I held my needs up to the last minute before I decided to go. But then there were another problem. The restrooms were very far from the classes. At the end of the huge corridor, or on another floor. Sometimes, I even had to use the elevator to get there.

Sadly, my power wheelchair was never really fast enough compared to my need to go. Once in a while, I wouldn't get there on time. It was so embarrassing! To dry my pants, I needed a blow dry job. I used the little machines meant to dry hands. I had to be creative. At the end of the year things got better, I was starting to totally control my body needs again.

One day in school, I managed to dodge getting a black eye. I was driving my power wheelchair somewhat distracted, and I bumped into a huge girl booty. She screamed and turned, with her fist ready to punch whoever did it to her. I got away by applying the old technique that the best defense is a good offense. I shouted as loud as I could:

"Hey, look where you a going! Can't you see me down here"? Everybody looked at her with a mad face. She was speechless and her angry face became angelic, and soon after, she apologized to me. I went from a run over villain to victim in two seconds! She did not know what really happened and ended up thinking it was her fault. That was close! I never saw her again. UFFA!

After graduation I was invited to return to school as a peer counselor assistant. My role in that class was to talk to troubled students telling my story and help them to believe they could overcome their challenges. It was very rewarding.

At that time, my social life was terrible as most of my friends had moved on with their lives. I was on my own. So, the position of peer counselor assistant turned out to be great for me. Having someone in the classroom that had gone through such a traumatic experience as mine, made the kids listen more attentively when the teacher spoke to them about the risks of using alcohol and drugs. I made a difference telling my classmates what doctors told me. "If I had any amount of any kind of drugs in my bloodstream, I would have died." Just talking to me, many of these kids realized that the problems in their lives that brough them to the peer counselor class weren't that tragic after all.

It was funny that I could be advising girls and boys. I had never been the best student in class or very obedient. I thought I would not be a good example to anyone. Nevertheless, I also never used drugs and I was never disrespectful to none of my teachers and colleagues. Maybe I could be a model to be followed.

Between school and therapies, life went on, but suddenly I started to miss a friend, one of the only two that kept around, the warrior; the dragon's lover, do you remember? So, I asked Rodrigo about him. And he told me that he was dating someone. I was surprised! Usually, he only got on with dragons, just to not fall in love.

I thought this time he had failed to escape from the beast, had died or was being held captive. But I was wrong! The situation was serious. He changed the patterns. He got a beautiful girl and was pleasant dominated.

About a month later, he showed up saying that his girlfriend's sister knew me from before the accident and would like to see me again.

He told me her name was Katia and how she looked like. I couldn't remember her at all, but the way he described her made me think that if I had really met her before I wouldn't have forgotten. He explained that she was a client of Casa Brazil, a Brazilian goods store that my family had for a year and where I have worked for few months. He also told me she used to go there almost every day to rent movies or books just to flirt with me. He went on saying - "She was in love with you, and you never noticed?"

I got curious. If she was the way he said- blonde, thin waist, smart, and a huge behind - I was very interested to meet her again. He said he would take me to her house soon. I accepted the invitation.

Two days later, Thiago picked me up to visit Katia around 6 pm. We had a great time remembering High School special moments, making jokes, talking silly, and eating a lot of snacks. We didn't even notice the time passing by. Suddenly it was already very late, and my friend grabbed his girlfriend's hand and said in a loud naughty voice: "I'm going to sleep with Keilinha, good night!" And he was gone.

I had been left alone with Katia and I had no way to get home. We looked around and to each other. I saw the sofa and started saying "I could sleep in …

Before I could finish what I was about to say (without much honesty, I confess), she said: "You can sleep in my room. My bed is a king-size and it can perfectly fit both of us." She smiled beautifully. It was not possible to decline that nice invitation. To the bad we went, and sleep was what we did. Believe me!

In the following weekend I repeated the visit. But this time I stayed over for the whole week. I have an explanation for that. At that time, my mother was already in Brazil and my father was finishing packing all of our things, Including our furniture. We were moving back there. For a few days we stayed in my sister's house. Of course, she wouldn't mind if I decided to spend my last days in Florida with Katia.

The week in Katia's house was going very well, but one day what I was always afraid of just happened. I needed to use the bathroom after breakfast, but her place had no adaptation for a wheelchair user, and Thiago had already left to work. I haven't said it yet, but he was a lifeguard at a nudist beach. The job was tough. He would endure a lot of sun, rain, wind and also the company of very old naked people. Thanks to God he was no longer a Warrior.

Well, as I was saying, I needed help to go to the bathroom. Katia did her best, but it was not enough. She did not have practice and wasn't strong enough. So, I fell. In seconds I was lying on the bathroom floor, naked and laughing so hard that I got cramps in my abs. The toilet was so close and yet so inaccessible. We got desperate. Katia could not help me, and I could not help myself. Any wrong effort could result in a worse situation.

To solve the problem, only a crane or her 6,7 feet tall neighbor. So embarrassing!

I enjoyed the experience of staying over Katia's house. Being with her was nice. She was 12 years older than me, But I always liked older girls, or I better say, more experienced.

I couldn't understand why I didn't remember her from our store, in the past. Could it have been possible that I had not noticed all that abundance? Maybe it happened because at that time I was dating Millie and couldn't even look at other girls. Katia told me that I probably never noticed her because she was chubby. I said, "no way", but thinking twice maybe she was right. I couldn't believe she was once fat.

Then she told me that her fine body was possible only after a liposuction. It ruined my self- image. Did I really care that much for appearances?

In addition to many others, she had a very special skill. She was a massage therapist. I received special and exclusive treatment, in addition to great kisses. We just clicked. Perfect.

As the old saying goes, all that is good short-lived. My time to return to Brazil was approaching.

She tried to change my mind by making an indecent proposal. She offered me a home to stay, food, laundry, and that irresistible massage for the rest of my life. I was very tempted to accept it. But discussing it calmly, we concluded that she had the right box for my truck, and more than that, together we formed a beautiful couple. We had a very good communion. But it was not the right time. It was hard, but I made up my mind: I took my truck without a box, and went by plane, back to Brazil.

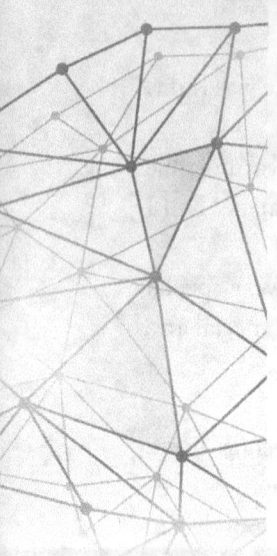

CHAPTER III

Back To Brazil

When we arrived in Brazil the Federal Police was on strike. At the airport it was already difficult. Long lines and a long time to wait. We were lucky that wheelchair users had priority in attendance. After about two hours we could go home.

My father had shipped our entire house to Brazil a week before. The international moving company had said that as soon as we arrived my father could clear our container through customs and hire a truck to take our things to Natal, where my mother was waiting for us. But we were spoiled. We had forgotten how things worked in the Third World.

In other circumstances, we wouldn't mind having to wait maybe two or three weeks for the strike to end. But not at that moment. Our entire house was inside a container stuck in the seaport of Fortaleza, a city eight hours' drive from where we intended to live.

Mom had traveled almost a month before us to choose a city in the northeast of Brazil and rent a house for us. For the time being, she was living in a small hotel on the beach. If all had gone well, when we arrived in Natal, the rented house would be available and the container with our things would be there just waiting for us. We would only have to unload the container and our house would be ready.

Nothing worked as we planned. The house my mom found and rented needed painting and cleaning and it was not available yet. The container with all of our belongings was still far away.

The solution would be to rent a room at the little hotel where Mom was staying and wait. We waited about a month.

The big problem at first were accessibility. Thanks to the friendship mom established with the owner she moved her office to the second floor and rented that room to accommodate me. It was a three-store build with no elevators. It wasn't that bad. The little hotel was right in Ponta Negra, the best beach in town.

The owner of the hotel was very friendly, as was everyone else working and hosted there. I was a kind of attraction. No one using a wheelchair had ever stayed in that hotel before. I became a kind of attraction. Everyone wanted to help me and hear my stories about America.

I wanted to meet girls, as always. For that I used to go to the bar in the lobby. There I saw one girl very special. Her name was Michele. A brunette. Black hair, long and straight, perfect body. On my third night there, she came to talk to me. Even her voice was sensual.

That was when the owner, who had already become a friend, covertly alerted me . She said: - "look carefully. She is beautiful but she is also an elephant". Surprised, I looked around and perceived the truth. She was a transvestite. The most beautiful I ever saw. She had the body and the grace of a young woman. Good thing I was warned before I tried to kiss her. She could deceive anyone.

One night our family went out for a stroll on the sidewalk. Our plan was to eat something and enjoy the moonlight and perfect temperature. That was when we found out how hard it was to be a tourist over there.

To start with, the restaurants were all very expensive, and tourists, especially from Europe, paid even more. Well, one Euro was worth almost four Reais. The extra charge really didn't matter.

We were not European tourists, but we were strangers in the area, I was using a power wheelchair not common there and my father, looked like a German: white hair and red face.

However, the fact that bothered us much was the huge number of children following us trying to sell everything:

pirated CDs, and videos, sunglasses, cheap jewelry, hats, beach clothes and even cell phones of suspicious origin. The same kind of stuff were also displayed on huge blankets in the middle of the sidewalk. We had to be caution not to trip on any artwork of all kinds. There were also sellers using costumes, no less famous than Madonna, Charles Chaplin, Michal Jackson, presidents of the USA and personages from Hollywood movies We met many Batmans, Pinguins, ETs and others.

On the street there were many food trucks and food cars, all with their own sound boxes playing very loud all kinds of music of all rhythms and nationalities, at the same time. Plus, the music coming from small wood carts full of CDs and hooked up with big speakers. Songs overlapped and trampled our ears. A horror party.

But not everything was bad. There were beautiful brunets, fascinating and charming blondies, nice people, amazing food, especially an incredible crepe, and a lovely beach and a magnific ocean view!

Finally, one day, after a lot of insistence, we received the key to the house we rented. However, despite all the time we waited for the landlord to paint and clean it, the house was nasty. The former tenants, all students, left there at least 4 hundred empty bottles of beer and other beverages, and about 3 hundred pounds of garbage: a couple of old and dirty mattresses, moldy sofas, broken shelves, and so on.

The house was big and facing the beach. Besides we would never know how much time it would take to find another house in that location. So, we decided to face the challenge. Clean and paint the whole house and keep it. We would finally have some privacy.

Three days of cleaning and painting, and some shopping, we would be more or less installed, although still without comfort. The Police federal strike was not over yet, and we still didn't have furniture. We were basically camping in the house for ten days.

We could not take it anymore. My father decided to go to Fortaleza and try to free our container.

During this period, we received an unexpected visit. We still didn't know anyone in town. A lady, and her son Juninho, came to our house looking for me. He was about nineteen years old. She explained that someone in her church had received a call from a girl in the United States, asking if the community could welcome a great friend and his family that just arrived in the city.

I was the great friend she mentioned and right away I identified Katia. Even so far away she was taking care of me. I was a blessed man!

Soon we met that lady's whole family. It was great! Juninho had two identical twin brothers one-year older than him, Levi, and Jonathan. They were both tall, handsome, and strong. At first it was very difficult to tell who was who. But once I got to know them better, it became easy. They were similar in appearance, but only Jonathan had worrier blood, just like my old friend Thiago.

They were very helpful too. If it wasn't for their strong arms and a few more friends that showed up , it would take 5 days just to unload the container my dad finally brought from Fortaleza.

Juninho was studying computer engineering at the University of Natal. He began helping us to install our computers and establish a house network. My mom ended up hiring him to help with our new online consulting business. Over time, he became part of my family, a son to my mom, and a brother to me.

I did not form a new quartet in Natal, but new friends arrived right on time. I was already going crazy.

Jonathan, one of the twins, called me one night: "Paulo, I'm here at the night club on the beach with two girls, but I can't understand a word they say. I think they are from Europe, Finland, I guess. Please, talk to them.

It was already past midnight when he called me, so I told him to bring them over. As soon as they arrived, I introduced myself, translated what Jonathan wanted to say and what they replied. And Jonathan and one of the girls went out onto the balcony to enjoy the full moon night.

They were on the hammock, doing their business despite not understanding what each other said. She had an injury on her mouth thar she said was a sunburn, but he didn't care. If it was herps he would be screwed, but they kept kissing and no longer needed a translator.

My luck never leaves me. Her friend was a white skin, blue eyes, and dark hair with a very familiar name to me, Catherine, which reminded me of the old days, before the accident. Besides, she were much better look than her friend.

Sneakily, we went to my room. On the contrary to the other Catherine, in USA, this time I was the one who didn't want to wake up my parents who were sleeping next door.

Everything was going fine until she asked me where I kept the condoms. I pointed out the drawer of my desk, but they were not there. I had given my last condom to Jonathan, thinking I would not be so lucky, especially because we had just met. I was wrong and I haven't given up. Barefoot and wrapped in a bed sheet, she went to the balcony to retrieve the condom packet from Jonathan. It would have solved the problem, but she returned without a solution.

Her friend ruined my plans reminding her of their pact - never have sex in that first visit to Brazil. I've never been so frustrated! I never saw those girls again and I heard from Jonathan that not long after that night, they went back to Finland.

Okay, that's life! If I went there, I would have solved it, but it was too much work, for me, to transfer in or out of the bed. So, I just let it go, very frustrated, but let it go! Never saw those girls again. Soon they went back to Finland.

Soon after the house was all fixed and cleaned, my grandfather also came to live with us. He was one of a kind: tall, with an athletic upper body. But nothing is always perfect, he had bird legs. He was so vain that the family had nicknamed him "the Baron". He always used Ralph Lauren starched shirts, linen pants, and a gold watch on his wrist. He was born in Brazil, but he was an American citizen and spoke good English.

On one occasion we went shopping for art crafts in the evening, and we decided to eat fried shrimp in a Bar, with live music, recently opened. To serve us came a tall, broad, and blond girl from Rio Grande do Sul , a Brazilian state all the way south of Brazil. She was about thirty-five years old, had a bright smile, a disposition to tell and hear histories, and was living alone in Natal. She did not stop looking at grandpa. Maybe she thought he was a rich "Lord."

To have a chance to get to him, Waldeth (the name of the blondie) decided she could be a great company for me. We scheduled to go to the beach the following Saturday. Thereafter, she always visited me, and we became great friends. She was an awesome girl. Cheerful, spontaneous, and helpful.

Before long, Waldeth's strategy worked out. The old man perked up, took a Viagra pill (he swore that he had never used) and called her to his room with an excuse to show her pictures on his computer. A while later, she came running and told me we would talk later, because she needed to go.

Later, on the phone, she told me my grandpa had tried to hit on her. She couldn't believe it. Her comment was at least funny: she said: "He still works, my God! I could kill him. He got me all wrong". Besides, the only thing I wanted was to take care of him the way I used to take care of old people back in my city.

I was surprised. My grandpa was hitting on my friends!

To keep me busy, while I didn't have a job, I signed up as a volunteer collaborator in a not-for-profit organization dedicated to rehabilitation of disabled people. There, I had the chance to meet new people and tell my experience of how life can be happy, even when facing so many difficulties and prejudices.

Among my new friends, I cannot forget two girls. The first was Fatima, a teacher and poet, deeply involved in the effort to help students and their families to find a reason to live and become integrated into society. She was the best example possible. She had multiple sclerosis, a deteriorating disease since childhood and was a forever user of a wheelchair.

As soon as we met, we decided to be a team. Joining forces, we began to develop a special project that she intended to implement at the organization. She would be the head, and I would be the public relations and the storyteller. For me it was the perfect function. Whoever knows me knows that I really enjoy talking. I feel great when I have an audience.

The other friend was a very special girl. She had a very severe disability. She was not able to talk, nor walk, she had an enormous spasticity (involuntary muscle contraction) that would prevent her to perform any of day-to- day regular activities. However, she was happy. She was always smiling and laughing. I've never before seen anyone able to express so much happiness and joy, with so little resources, mentally and physically. I became her number one fan. I named her super Mirna.

As I was always at the Organization, they invited me to help them during the International Assistive Technology Fair, which would take place at the Natal Convention Center. I loved the invitation, it was a chance to meet more people.

My job was to help communicate with visitors who only spoke English. I worked very little, not because I did not want to, but because there were just few foreigners. But I had a great time.

Toward to the end of the event, I went for a spin in my wheelchair, and I saw a girl playing a guitar and singing well in English, a song I knew from the heart. I stopped immediately and started singing with her. We were interpreting Sugar Ray, Smash Mouth, Shaniya

Twain, among others. How could I? Everyone knows I'm very out of tune.

Here, I have to confess that I do not know why she did not ask me to stop singing. I'm sure I was messing it up. Luckily for me she realized that bad singers also have a heart. Words of the famous Brazilian compositor and singer -Tom Jobim.

I was grateful and dying to flirt again. Of course, I did not miss the opportunity and invited her to do something together soon: go to a restaurant, watch a show, a game or go to the movies.

Without surprise, she accepted. (yeah, I was still good at that game). We went out on a date, and had some fun, for a while. But she was only eighteen. Nothing wrong with that, but always liked older women, remember?

But she made a difference when she told me that a local university had a physical therapy facility where students received practical classes for anyone in need. I went there and sign up for literally be a guinea pig. Nothing could be worse than not to have therapy.

On the first day, I was pleasantly surprised. The place was huge, had excellent equipment and a lot of teachers. It was a place that I could call heaven, or purgatory. It all depended on the teacher's selection of who would be dealing with me.

My chances were good. There were thirty nice girls and only seven guys. But I was a little worried. After all I'm not short or skinny. I'm 5'10 of pure muscle. (not all of them were working, though). My concern was not all the girls could handle me.

I got lucky again. Instead of one, I got two wonderful girls: They were kind, fun and great professionals.

Doing therapy there was like a double dose of treatment. Besides rehab for my legs and arms I also had eyes treatment.

After all, seeing so many pretty girls is more effective than eye drops.

Each quarter it started all over: new class, new teachers, and new students. Early in the second year, I was sure I would get new cute girls to work with me. Taking a good look at all the students, I had made a secret choice about which one I wanted. I just needed a little bit of luck. This time my luck failed.

From that day on, I was only designated to male physiotherapists. Some evil tongues said it was a course from some of my dissatisfied girlfriends. It was a lie. All of my exgirlfriends became my friends.

It was cruel to see the cute therapists from a distance. As much as I understand the importance of keeping to the ethical rules, and never thought of getting involved with my therapists, I undoubtedly preferred to be assisted by the girls. The hands of the guys made me itch a lot. I'm totally allergic to male's touch.

Going to therapy twice a week and rolling my chair on Ponta Negra beach sidewalk was good, but I wanted to go back to school and also start working. I needed to think ahead. So, I signed up for an eight-month Travel Agent course at SENAC. Tourism was booming in the area.

After high school in the US, it was the first time I entered a classroom. I was not sure if I was ready to read and remember so many handouts and try higher levels of education including math. However, I would never know if I was ready or not without trying it.

It was worth every minute! The class was not large, although it was very diverse. There were people of every race, age, sex, and temperament, good for every taste. I was very unique in that class. I was the only one who had an exclusive chair and a desk (My desk was attached to my power wheelchair). I was soon accepted by everyone in the school.

Almost every night after the course, I had to wait for my father to pick me up. There were always a lot of people there waiting for someone. But sometimes there was only one girl sitting alone on one of the benches.

One night we started talking, so the time would pass faster. We talked a lot, and little by little, we started feeling attracted to each other. I knew what I felt and saw the same in her eyes.

She was tiny, well done little body, and had yummy lips, so good! That gloss lipstick she always wore was a temptation. One day I could not resist it, and I suddenly kissed her. (Stolen kisses are always better).

What a terror! That little and attractive mouth was like a carnivorous plant. She almost swallowed me and my chair all at once! Inhac! . In the following days, I only pop kissed her. I was still afraid! I do not know what I told her, but I decided to stay, without kissing for a while, I was traumatized! After I finished the course, I never saw her again. I remembered the SENAC (the name of the institution where we were studying), as "SEE --- INHÁC"!

A little bit before the end of the course, I overcame the trauma. I became involved with a blonde girl in my class. She was very nice and very cute, but not very bright. She lived relatively close to my house. I even thought that finally I would have a nice relationship, at least without risk. But I do not think I was very good at future predictions. Once again, I was wrong.

She was the type of 0.8 or 8000, which mean everything or nothing. Soon, she came with that crazy talk. "Are we going to be together to get married soon, or just hook up, with no commitment? I didn't want to get married under pressure like that. For me, Love had to happen first. We had our fun! But other things did not click well. We became friends. That was it.

To live by the beach has its advantages. The view was fantastic and the people there, strolling or working, lived in a special little world, without any rush, they were happy and relaxed all the time.

At night, this atmosphere was even more pleasant. That was when the conversations got excited without commitments, and the storytellers put together memories and fantasies, reality, and fiction. That's when the boys told their advantages and achievements to friends and girls who pretended to believe. Everyone was happy. Those were some of the most fun moments!

Thus, almost every night I went down to the beach sidewalk. My favorite destination was a mini store, where tourists bought Buggy rides to explore the dunes. While there, the riders told me all kinds of stories. Each one was more unbelievable than the next. We used to spend hours talking and laughing. I also told them my stories. Some are in this book now, and some others can't ever be written.

Everything was falling in place again, but I was missing one thing that I've being away for a while. It was when I met Rose.

A friend invited me to visit her church in the area of Capim Macio. A city very close to the city I was living in. She told me she had many friends that she wanted to introduce to me. Rose was one of them. It was a connection at first sight. My crushes on mouths made me super, hyper, mega vulnerable. I immediately invited her for ice cream. She suggested we go to the mall at the beach. Great choice, I also wanted to visit the place.

At that moment we were at the higher stage of flirting. She was eight years older than me, the way I like it.

On the table of the bar and restaurant, each one on opposite sides, examined the menu. I began trying to choose the entrée, since most of the things on the menu I'd never heard about before. I asked her to choose for us. She did. "let's go for a typical Northeast of Brazil flavor- Sururu. Saying this word she spoke with a very sensual voice, looking straight to my eyes. Her lips were like a small bird's beak. She also said: "You are going to love it". The brownish eyes, and those magnificent, beautiful lips saying SURURU, sounded more than suggestive to me.

Then, we had to choose our drinks. I told her that I always want to try different flavors, preferably sweet and sour, just like life. In a hot night and close to the beach, I wanted some refreshing juice. So, she asked me if I knew mangaba. Of course, I didn't! "Oh! It is a delicious berry, with a peculiar characteristic". Do you want to try it? I was curious and asked for some more information, just to see her lovely and tempting mouth moving and her playful expression showing with her lips the effect of drinking mangaba's juice.

She made another beak, cuter than the first one, and started closing and opening her lips continuously. It looked like a goldfish. Again, an invitation to kiss. I've got the message and went for it. It was sweet and yummy.

The pleasant company and the sweet kisses got me all the way. I was dating again. It happened naturally. Our feelings were flowing.

Miraculously, she showed me a way to go back to God's path. Soon, I was integrated into the youth group at the church she attended and met good new friends.

We had a super healthy relationship. We dated about eight months or so, and we never had a fight. It was only joy. She knew I liked dark skin girls, and secretly wore little or no sunscreen when we went to the beach. She always burned in the sunlight, but she couldn't get darker than bright pink. However, she tried!

I've liked her a lot, but I do not know why, every time, when I looked at my future, wouldn't see her as my wife, only a good, dear friend. I decided to tell her that and we stopped dating, but we maintained the great friendship and affection we had, which lasts until today.

The course at SENAC was over, but I needed to study more to achieve my professional dreams. When I still lived in the US, I wanted to become a lawyer. However, in Brazil it no longer seemed so attractive. No one deserves to live in a suit and wear a tie all day long in the "land of the sun". The nickname of Natal was really appropriate.

My better option was going to the University to get a bachelor's degree in Tourism and hospitality.

At that time the profession was in evidence since tourism in Natal was benefited from the high value of the euro and the dollar. For me, the Tourism degree would be perfect because I was fluent in English and also could speak enough Spanish to communicate. It certainly would be my positive differential.

On the Internet, I looked for offers of that course. My criteria to choose the right Institution involved credibility, house proximity and price. Through phone calls I began to receive information on how to participate in the selection process to be accepted. That's where my problems started.

On my first attempt, the selective program coordinator explained that I should write a page about a specific topic. That would be easy for me! But he offered me only a blank sheet of paper and a thin pen. They wouldn't' allow me to use a computer. Besides, I would have only thirty minutes to finish the task.

In an instant I went from over confident to terrified. Due to the brain damage resulting from my motorcycle accident, my hand coordination was poor and as a result, my cursive handwriting was sometimes illegible. I couldn't write in a straight line either. I'm sure I've written a good argumentative text, as they asked, but I knew even I couldn't read my composition. I failed. Maybe being in that school would not be good for me. As I always say, nothing happens without God's will.

While enduring my big disappointment, on a Sunday afternoon, I got a visit from a family friend. He was accompanied by a girl who fortunately, was a teacher in a college nearby. Conversing, I talked about the sad experience that made me lose the chance to enter college and I complained that people talk a lot about social inclusion and accessibility but do too little about it. I was surprised when she said: "Why don't you try UNIFACEX? I'm sure they will treat you much better."

In the very next day, I called that University to schedule the entrance exam. But this time I made myself clear explaining I was a physical disabled person, and I needed a computer.

My first contact was very positive. They provided a computer for my entrance test and also assured me the college was offering good accessibility to all academic environments and they also would do their best to address any students' needs. Using a computer, it was too easy! I was accepted.

I will never forget the years I studied at UNIFACEX. The classes were small, but there were always events to integrate all the students of several fields. Soon, I felt I had a huge family.

Like every family, we had all kinds of colleagues. Some were clearly the lazy type, others were tricksters, envious, jealous, formals, boring or always in a bad mood. But many were funny, kind, helpful, smart, sweet, and beautiful, especially the girls.

Some teachers also made history: one of them was a sex symbol according to all the girls, another thought he was, and there wasn't a single student that wouldn't give an A (nothing more academic), to a certain gorgeous professor.

Field trips were special events of revelation and mutual understanding. Some of them entered the story of the university and are unforgettable.

The most comical thing I remember happened on the bus when we were arriving at UniFacex after visiting a historic city close to Natal.

One of our friends stuck his head out the window and shouted to a girl who just got off the bus: "I love you Byparmá" The friendly girl's nickname related to the city where she lived- Parnamirim. But the answer he received came unexpectedly from a car parked on the side of the bus: "Did you lose your mind? What are you talking about?" It was his wife, who had come to surprise him. Everybody teased him for a long time.

The scariest thing that happened during one of our fieldtrips occurred one afternoon when we were gathering on the bus to return to Natal after a day in a quiet country town where we went to verify why that city was known as the most peaceful in the state.

Almost everyone was already on the bus except two students, when we heard three loud "booms" that sounded like gunshots. Looking from the bus windows we saw a lot of people running around and screaming. Our professor immediately got off the bus to look for the missing students. We all breathed a sigh of relief when we saw the two guys running to the bus.

Still a little scared they said that a man died from three shots to his chest, at close range. However, the reasons were still a mystery. Some spoke of revenge for some betrayal, others said that the cause was probably a woman or debts. The city's radio station was already broadcasting the incredible bad news. So much for a peaceful city! Our research was already meaningless.

On one occasion, our group participated in a survey about the gay's movement, the most promising emerging market niche in the tourism field at the time. It was an opportunity to pay attention to students and professors around us and train our capacity to identify the ones that never came out of the closet. Some students were experts in the subject. The bets on some colleagues and professors were high. But it was hard to be sure! No one could really tell. But we knew!

BEWARE WHAT YOU WISH FOR!

I was still in the fourth semester when my mother, coming back from João Pessoa, capital of Paraíba, another state in the Northeast of Brazil, but only about two hours driving from Natal, said to me: Maybe I met a girl who perfectly matches the description you made about the ideal woman for you".

She knew it was the right introduction to awaken my attention and rouse my curiosity. She got me thinking, but I was not very excited about. The girl lived too far away. Besides, mom might have exaggerated a little. So, I tried not to think much about it. But one day, when I got home after a normal busy day, I saw an extremely interesting girl sitting in my living room. As soon I saw her, I knew right away she was the girl from the other state my mother had told me about. .

She was way better than my mom had said or of what I could have ever imagined: black, long straight hair, beautiful, deliciously fine, and smart. She also still filled the prerequisite that Dad had added to my ideal perfect girl: She had to be a physical therapist or a nurse. She was a nurse! I freaked out all the way!

Unfortunately, she wasn't there to meet me. She had come to my home to talk business with my mom!

I could do nothing but wait. As it got really late for her to drive back home, my mother suggested that it would be safer to sleep in our house. The next day she could even go to the beach and return to João Pessoa after lunch. I still tried to be kind and offered my room for her to sleep, but it did not work, she chose to make her bed on the floor of the office room we had. What a waste! I Barely slept that night, thinking about her!

At dawn, I got out of bed extremely hyper, totally alert. I was so excited that made people jealous! She would be leaving our house that afternoon. I did not have much time, I needed to do something! I was sure she was the one capable to make me really get over my first true love.

Finally, after the beach and lunch, we could talk more privately. I almost blew it! Actually, I did. I was so nervous that she even thought I had mental problems. It was a fiasco! I couldn't even remember to get her phone number, or any other kind of communication. Perhaps have I lost all my player games. (I had no idea what happened to me).

I had to appeal to Mom. Of course, she had all the information I needed, since Dafna was her client. But she decided to play tough and said: _"Paulo, I cannot give it to you, it is unethical". I almost cried!

Then, she said she would send Dafna a message asking for permission. It was all I had, a very little tine light at the end of the tunnel! Better than nothing right?

Later on, my mother gave me her MSN information. I wanted to jump, run, dance… and do all crazy stuff, but I remembered that I was still in a wheelchair. So, I came down and started to think how to make my sixth first love happen. I think this is the sixth, right? To someone to fall in love with me now is not as easy as used to be before the accident. Adding to that, her first impression of me might have been not really good! I knew this time everything would be different. I was already older, and I knew exactly who I was, what I wanted and how I wanted. I wanted her, she would be the girl of my life! I would find the way to her heart.

Our relationship happened slowly. She took over a week to accept my invitation on MSN. That little light at the end of the tunnel was already fading away. But finally, that light shined stronger when she answered. It renewed my hope.

However, there were still other problems. She lived over a hundred miles away. What a terrible feeling! Everything was too hard. What could I do? I can't control my heart!

Gradually, Dafna and I were talking and strengthening our bounds, unfortunately it was virtually only. We talked for hours on MSN and phone every day, until my mother told me that she would have to return to our home to bring some documents and sign a contract. It was my chance. I would have a second chance, and maybe my last!

Now I knew the day she would come and even the approximate time. I planned a master risky strategy, and I armed the trap. I bought several red roses and a bouquet of pink roses with red tips. With the petals of the red roses, I made a path that ended in my room. Where I was holding the other bouquet waiting for her.

When the doorbell rang, I knew it was her, but I did not answer it. I asked Mom to tell her to follow the path of red petals, and that is it, nothing more. And I warned my mother not to say that I was with my four tires completely flat for her. It could ruin everything. A man cannot be too vulnerable, girls are dangerous!

My strategy worked. With that kind of welcoming reception, what woman could resist? The first kiss happened right there in the middle of the roses. I can't forget the firm and delicious lips of that beautiful black woman finally touching mine. It had been years since I kissed a black girl. I do not know why. I always loved it.

It was more than amazing that we fell in love very fast in such a way that every time we were together kissing or not, sparks were everywhere. We had to be careful not to burn places. I wanted to spend the rest of my life with that girl, for sure. For the first time, I wasn't thinking of Millie as much!

People say that long distance relationship does not work, but we tried. We were together for one weekend, and we would be longing to see each other for three weeks. Somehow it peppered our relationship.

We'd been together for about six months when one afternoon, out of the blue, we started talking about marriage and plans for the future. I explained to her, I would love to take our relationship one step further, but for me it was still complicated at that time. I was still a student, with four semesters to go, and I did not even have a chance to meet her parents.

I Remember like it was twenty years ago, since my longterm memory is much better than the short term one. She looked into my eyes and said, playing mad. _ "are you just thinking, yet" ?

I was speechless. Women are just like that! While we men are going, they have been, have returned and are already going again. I will not deny that I was surprised with that answer ... and also delighted. But I did not say when or where I would make the proposal, but I decided to use the opportunity to go to her house on her birthday to meet her parents and ask for their daughter's hand in marriage.

My parents and I arrived at her house early on her birthday. Her party would happen at night. I used our early arrival as an opportunity to talk to her parents one at a time. First, I talked to her mother. She would be easier to convince, but maybe more difficult to get along with. Mother-in-law, you know it. Then, I went to talk to her father, a man who was a Military Police Colonel and looked like Dino from the Dinosaur Family, a TV show. He was very friendly. He said: _ "Paulo, you and my daughter are adults, and it seems like you both know what you want, I wouldn't go against it." I was relieved. It went better than I expected.

It was already getting dark, and l had it all planned. The box of the engagement rings was a rosebud, which I put in the middle of a bouquet I had bought for her.

In the middle of the party, I borrowed the microphone from the keyboard player, and I began my speech. At first, I pleased her mother with some pretty words and a bouquet of country flowers. Then, I thanked her parents for their kindness and when our preferred song started in the background, I made the proposal in English, the way she desired.

I couldn't rely on the keyboard player to translate my speech. Every sentence I spoke, he invented a funny version in Portuguese. It was comical! But it worked fine, she said yes and kissed me. I loved watching her friends crying. Were they all envious? Her divine smile made my day. It was undoubtedly a moment to remember for a lifetime.

Unlike here, in Brazil men and women wear engagement rings in their right hands. So, after the kissing I was ready to put the ring on her finger, but I noticed she was already wearing it. And surprisingly, so was I. How did she get it on my hand? I didn't see it happening! She was fast!

At first, our relationship was even hotter. The engagement rings were beautiful in our hands. Everyone was wondering when the wedding would be. But I couldn't answer it. I had not yet finished school, and my income in dollars was shrinking. My financial situation was going from stable to a little complicated. The dollar value was going down fast. I was in trouble.

The money difficulty, however, was just the beginning of the end. She, who always came to my city to spend four or five days with me every fifteen days, started to come only one weekend a month. Despite the fact that we were still capable of having fun together, it was not the same anymore.

Until one day, chatting, she let slip she expected her future husband to earn more than she did at that time. Besides she wanted to get married before her thirtieth birthday. She was already twenty-six years old and a certified nurse.

I got the message. The dollar was very low, I hadn't even graduated yet, and I had a shitty part time job at a hotel, earning little more than minimum wage, because school was my priority. Little hours, short money, and an annoying job that wasn't challenging at all. However, I enjoyed going to work. I met some very interesting people, nice, cute girls, and others, maybe not co cute, but really fun. I even made good friend at this hotel, especially a young woman who had the same function as mine. People were gossiping that we were lovers, and we pretended to be flirting just to increase their curiosity. We had so much fun. The camaraderie between colleagues and the manager's friendly attitude helped the time pass and even made up a little for the meager salary.

I told Dafna, that I was in a transitional moment. That I would have to wait two more years to graduate before I could get a better job with more adequate payment.

It is always possible to make good money in the hotel business, but it takes time and a lot of experience. She was right. Her waiting time would be long. I wasn't even sure if I wanted to be a hotel manager. Honestly, this wasn't my plan at all. I always dreamt of opening my own business and being my own boss. Decidedly, my reality did not match her expectations.

Dafna wasn't happy. She insisted that she needed more than possible good perspectives, she needed to be sure she would have a comfortable lifestyle, and she could not see that in our future. The point was our passion was over. I felt our engagement was about to end. She no longer came to visit me. She never returned my phone calls and messages. Silence.

One morning I called her from a phone she didn't know. She answered. We had a serious conversation and I never saw her again. I finally understood she wanted to break our engagement for some time but didn't have the courage to take the initiative.

I haven't dropped a tear or showed sadness during our last phone conversation, but after hanging up I cried compulsively, ridiculously. It was the end of one more dream. I had lost my sixth or seventh first love. Who is counting? I was devastated. I spent all morning remembering and crying, remembering, and crying. At bath time I hardly needed a shower. I was already wet. After all, shower and bed were our preferred places in the house. It was hard to bear the idea of lack of company in those especial places.

Towards the afternoon, I began to have more practical ideas. Perhaps changing my bed? Or my wheelchair, where we many times... rode together? Or my clothes, which had been rubbed on her? On second thought, I realized everything would bring good memories but if I got rid of everything, I would have also have to change my...! A few weeks later, one night, I made-up my mind: "I'm going to sleep because tomorrow will be a better day". In the morning, I woke up ready to start over! It was a pity. All of my ex-girlfriends were still my friends, except Dafna, who was the only one who had ever been my fiancé. I was very disappointed! I never saw her again.

OVERCOMING AND SWEAT

I was already training table tennis in a not-for-profit organization named SADEF for almost a year when suddenly my coach invited me to attend the Paralympics Brazil Table Tennis Cup that would happen in João Pessoa, my ex's fiancé hometown.

Despite knowing that I wasn't good enough yet to attempt a tournament, I accepted.

It was my first competition and of course I wanted to win. In my category were only five competitors including one of my teammates, Tercio, who always beat me in training games. The other three players were from other states. Because I am a very lucky man, I won my first match by W/O. There were four more matches to reach the gold.

On the following games I won some sets, but never an entire game, which led me to compete for third place. I was somewhat frightened because my opponent was just my teammate Tercio, against whom I never scored a set. I could not escape from it and decided to fight the best way I could. I don't know what happened, but I ended up winning the game. I returned home holding a bronze medal. Tercio was totally upset, very angry and confused. How did this happen?

I could not answer that question either. Did I embody the spirit of some Chinese player? Maybe Tércio was on sleep pills? Detail: A year later, I still couldn't win a single game against him. But I never let him forget my victory. I would be the best in tournaments.

About 5 months later, we were competing again in the Brazilian Championship in Fortaleza. This time everything went sore. To start with, they reclassified me. I was in class two, for people with major disabilities and they relocated me to class five. The highest class before the one for players that could play standing up.

The error occurred because the new classification was based on spinal cord injuries, which cause the difficulties presented by paraplegics. I had no spinal cord injuries. So, they could not classify me properly. I did not have a chance! But my friend, who wanted revenge, couldn't get his chance against me. He was permanently a class two player. However, not everything was bad. The hotel was great, there was good food, and the best thing was to be among friends.

On the night after the games, we decided to go eat something in a beach bar. Nothing special to celebrate, just one of us got a bronze medal. But to commemorate we did not need a reason. My friends liked to drink beer. I can't say the same, but being with them drinking fruit juices, talking, and laughing reminded me of old times.

Suddenly, one of our friends got up and left for no apparent reason. Shortly after, he returned with two girls. I thought he was already drunk or high when he said: "I brough two pieces of filet mignon to keep us company" referring to the girls accompanying him. By the looking of the girls, I was sure he was a good goldsmith, but he certainly had no knowledge about meat. I somehow admired him. He was a man with a lot of courage. A true warrior.

Between table tennis practice and college, I was very busy, but of course, I could get some free time for dating. I needed to find another love. But who? Among so many beautiful girls that were circulating at the university, it would be difficult to choose. My luck was that, in fact, I didn't have to choose. Girls are the ones who chooses. They have this power. I was soon chosen by a cute girl, with a lovely smile and timid eyes. She was blond, petit and was studying to be a nurse. She would fit perfectly in my arms. She seemed fragile, so I approached her slowly and gently. We got to know each other, and we fell in love in no time.

Unfortunately, our relationship didn't go too far. At first, I believed it ended because of her shyness, especially because she required secrecy about our relationship. Then, I realized it was more than that. She was ashamed of herself. She didn't believe she could awaken the love of any man.

Her problem was exclusively because of a small swivel in her spine that made her limp a little when walking. She was beautiful and intelligent, but never believed that her different walking seemed charming to my eyes. I don't understand, I could not walk at all.

My problem was that I could not keep a secret about dating her because there is no reason to hide what gives me a lot of joy and was also good for the body and soul.

I was beginning to feel it would be difficult to find true love for life. But I would not give up yet! I would only have to postpone my plans to marry early and have children while I am young. I thought it would be good to have a lot of disposition to play with them, understand and be like a friend to them.

My time in the University was about to end and I still hadn't managed to motivate my colleagues to throw a big farewell party. I had been trying for a while. I was successful when I suggested a costume party at my house.

At this time, I was living in a big house with an even bigger backyard, excellent for parties. Although it happened in October, it would have nothing to do with Halloween, witches, and ghosts. The idea was that each could wear the costume they wanted.

The result was "the night of revelations." We had go-go boys, transvestites, babies, clowns, pirates, vampires and even a priest, that should not be too Catholic, because he lost his wedding ring in a pool match. Let me explain. He lost his ring while playing, because he took it off to play better. He did not bet on it.

The girls were also creative. We saw fairies, witches, princesses, prisoners, escort girls, little devils, and a Maria Bonita. She was the wife of a legendary personage of the most arid land in the northeast of Brazil. Loved by the poor people and hated by landowners. A bandit and a rescue angel.

Of course, not everything was as expected. The go-go boy inexplicably pulled only "males" to dance, despite making the greatest success with all the ladies, wearing only a bathing suit and a bow tie. He was hilarious.

The vampire was defeated by a pirate faster on the gun trigger to protect Maria Bonita from the gruesome bite.

The next day, almost seven in the morning, my mother had to start kicking some booties out. The worse one was the vampire. It was difficult to dislodge him from our living room couch. After all, vampires sleep when the day rises.

The balance of the party was extremely positive. The mood among colleagues got even better. And, of course, I couldn't miss talking about Maria Bonita, the cangaceira, whose real name was Cristiane.

THE PIRATE AND THE MARIA BONITA

Cristiane wasn't my classmate. She was studying Social Science on the night shift. I used to stay late after my afternoon classes waiting for my ride to take me home. One of those nights we met, and after a while we became good friends. It's obvious I had other intentions.

Later, I found out that she was targeting me for a year before we officially met. How could I have never noticed her? It was probably possible because I was always surrounded by a lot of people or maybe she was too discreet. She was beautiful. Black hair, very yummy mouth, a stunning smile, an attractive body, and a lovely voice. She was a little bit older than me. Just the way I liked.

At first, I was so fascinated by the way she was: nice, kind, caring, friendly and always in a good mood, just like me, that I didn't even bother to look at her body. A had a chance when we said goodbye and we walked away in opposite directions. Then, I decided to look back to check her out. Wow! Her waist, hips, legs, and everything in between were just perfect. How could I have never noticed her before? Maybe I spent all those years in the University flirting or dating the wrong girls. But it meant nothing now. The "before" was in the past. I wanted to live in the present and maybe in the future. With her? I invited her to my party.

She showed up to my party by herself. She was wearing boots almost to the knees, a dagger knife at her waist (dangerous!), a skirt up to her thighs and a typical "cangaceira" hat. She was way more beautiful than everyone else.

"cangaceira" - A women part of the armed group that roamed the hinterland of Northeast Brazil, at the end of the 19th century. Lampião was the leader. His wife was Maria Bonita.

The party was rolling on and I, despite giving attention to everyone, just thought of her. Therefore, I kept her constantly observed from a certain distance, not to show a lot of interest, covertly. It was when I saw a vulture vampire, flying lower and getting too close, even though I knew he wouldn't be a real threat to me at all, I decided to be safer than sorry. I got closer and started a private conversation.

To my surprise, she immediately whispered in my ear: "Paulo this vampire is following me everywhere I go. I don't know what to do". I said: "relax, I will take care of it". She began to tell me not to say anything to him, but before she finished her sentence, I surprised her with a kiss. One act works better than a thousand words. I had sent a loud and clear message that reached the target perfectly. When we finished kissing, the vulture vampire had flown away.

At that moment we began our romance. She became my "Princess" but at home, I called her "cangaceira".

A little bit after that amazing party, our class would be doing a road trip to Seridó, our last field trip, to finish our research about the tourist cities in the State. It would also be part of our graduation package, instead of having a party.

Usually, my constant mate on those trips was my dad, to help me with transfers and whatever else I needed. Of course, he loved those chances to go sightseeing with the excuse that he had to help me. However, this time he was dismissed. I invited Cristiane to come with me. No one could take their companions, and nobody wanted it either. We would have no privacy, as four of us would sleep in the same room. Luckily, I needed a special adapted room for disabled for me and my companion, whoever would assist me. Perfect! Although ultra-worried, my dad accepted the arrangement, but only after repeating a million recommendations. Well, he had no other choice.

Even with all my classmates around, I could only perceive her and I, nothing else mattered. Time stopped! All the affection she showed, all her care and interest in learning how to deal with my disabilities, and her pure and giving attitude and simplicity, made me believe again in real love for life.

That two-day trip was perfect. She was exactly what I expected and wanted for my life. We dated for about four months, completely in love. But unfortunately, we did not know how to deal with one very important issue. - Religion. As the saying goes, "everything that is good, short lived". She wasn't yet my love for lifetime. What a pity!

Finally, the classes ended. But before we all went different ways, we planned a special event. - The "Class to remember." We gathered at the University auditorium. We had a lot of fun pretending we were in a real graduation ceremony, acknowledging some talents and offering colleagues, funny diplomas that expressed specific characteristics of each one. The one with the highest grades received a Mr. Nerd diploma. The diploma of Mr. Mayor was given to a classmate who aspired to be a politician. I've got a Mr. Congeniality diploma, of course. We awarded other colleagues with Mr. Tourist - he was seldom in class. Mr. Maniac, who was hard to deal with because he could never change his mind. Very intransigent. Mr. impoverished, that was always whining, and many others of the genre.

Not even the professors escaped. We should not forget Mr. jungle, which also was known as ninja turtle Donatello. Mr. Diogenes earned his nickname for his fixation with a writer with that name. If there were also other nicknames, I'd rather not say it.

MR SIMPATIA (Mr. Congeniality)

A NEW MOMENT

When I finished University, our family decided to go back to the USA after nearly four years away from there. It was a great experience. It was time to catch up with the family and some old friends, that I had been contacting only by internet. Several things have changed during my absence.

As soon as I arrived, I was invited to Rodrigo's wedding ceremony. Rodrigo, my faithful friend that was a member of my last quartet of true friends. He was getting married, the wedding was beautiful, but I wasn't his best man, because nobody knew if I was going to be around.

I also had a chance to go to the one-year birthday of my sister's youngest son. I played a lot with My brother Fábio's son, who was a redhead only ten months old. A big surprise was to meet Millie's daughter. Even more surprising than that was to hear from her mother- the one that has made our lives miserable "It would have been way better if Millie was with you". I thought *"of course it would be better. I loved her unconditionally. I would do everything to make her happy."* I haven't said a word, but I kept thinking that not being an Argentinian would already be better for her. Hahaha!

Back in Brazil I found on the internet a girl who have worked with me at the NGO doing some voluntary work for more than two years. At that time, we only bumped into each other at the facility and said HI, unpretentiously (very different from that HI I mentioned at the beginning of this book). We never had a chance to talk. We were always in a rush.

One afternoon, we decided to go for a walk-Well, you know my walk. Maybe we could eat something and get to know each other better. There was when I met her little daughter, a beautiful child, very charming. It was the beginning of a nice friendship. No malicious thoughts involved. I enjoyed have her around and I wouldn't let any sexual attraction ruin it.

Meanwhile, I was flirting with a new girl. I couldn't understand when she got mad because I went out, as a friend, with that other girl and her little daughter. She wasn't even my girlfriend yet. Why was she so jealous, causing a tsunami in a drop of water? It made me notice that she was boiling me in cold water, but she didn't want me to get involved with anyone else. It looked like she was measuring forces. She even commented: _ "She already has a daughter, and you love children so I'm at a disadvantage…"Of course, I want kids, but I want to have my own". Right there she said she would fulfil my dream. Who would ever understand women's head?

To make a long story, short, two years later I married with that woman. She was also a permanent disabled, user of a wheelchair. I did everything right, I worked hard, I bought a house, I was always present, I respected and got along greatly with her family. I was a good husband. But the kids never happened.

Our relationship came to an end when I found out she wasn't just postponing pregnancy. She was avoiding it, secretly taking anti-conception pills. She never wanted to have children. I felt deceived.

My father always warned me not to think of myself as a romantic lunatic. Whenever it comes to women issues, relationships, and things from the heart, he always reminded me of what he says all the time: _ "every man is a full when it comes to women." I think he's damn right, especially when we like them!

EPILOGUE

Well, so that was my childhood, adolescence, and a good part of my twenties. From great joys to irreparable losses, I was shaping a new way of seeing life.

I've always been optimistic, curious, and adventurous, but now, to all of that I add prudence and appreciation of the great little things in life.

From girls to girls, over the years, I have been perfecting the technique of been happy and making them happy, at least while it lasts. But now, it's no longer a time to remember the past- romances, love affairs, uncontrollable passions, fiascos, and successes.

Now is the time to look at the future ,make new choices and hope they are right. It's time to seek professional fulfillment and independence to start with, and then, when the time comes, my love for life will happen naturally. Until then I will keep selecting what to remember to live better. Since I believe we are what we remember.

Paulo Castro

ABOUT THE AUTHOR

Paulo V. Castro was born in Rio de Janeiro. Brazil, in 1982. In 1998. he left forthe United States. His parents reunited after fifteen years of being apart.

Thanks to the teachings of life: family love and problems, studies, and diverse experiences, he learned to value being it, instead of having it!

His weaknesses were caused by a traumatic brain injury prior to his senior year in high school that affected his short-term memory and turned him into a permanent wheelchair-user. However, those never defined him. He acknowledged them and learned to surpass the difficulty and pursue his objectives in life.

A few years after the accident, he finished high school. He now holds diplomas in teaching, entertainment, and travel from FACEX University in Brazil and a bachelor's degree in psychology from Keiser University in Florida, United States.

Coping with an eventful and challenging youth, he discovered writing as a therapy and a pleasure.